# BUSH TRACKS
# OF
# VICTORIA

## 25 Great 4WD Adventures

**A Kakirra Adventure
Guide**

# BUSH TRACKS OF VICTORIA

**Published by:** Kakirra Adventure Publications,
PO Box 112,
Pearcedale. Vic.
Australia 3912.
Phone/Fax: (059) 787 066

**Typeset by:** Abb-Typesetting Pty Ltd,
Collingwood, Victoria.

**Printed by:** Brown Prior Anderson,
Burwood, Victoria.

**Photographs by:** Ron & Viv Moon (unless otherwise stated).

**Maps by:** Ron & Viv Moon (unless otherwise stated).

**This Edition:** 1st Edition, October 1990.
2nd Edition, October 1993.

**National Library of Australia card number and ISBN 0 9588264 2 0**

**© Ron & Viv Moon, 1990.**

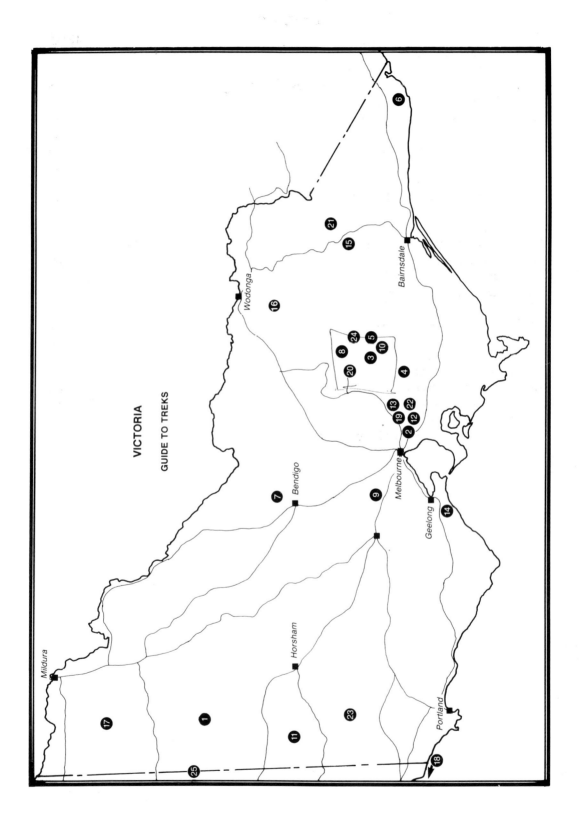

VICTORIA

GUIDE TO TREKS

# CONTENTS

5

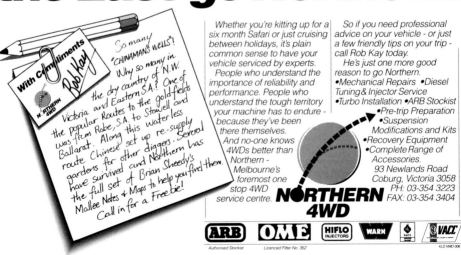

# INTRODUCTION ... AND A WORD OF ADVICE

In the twelve months it has taken us to compile this book we've had more fun, excitement and plain sheer old fashioned enjoyment than we've had for ages. It's taken us into areas we've known little about and we've been amazed and delighted at the breadth and depth of the outdoor experience that Victoria can offer. It really is a state that has everything.

The treks in this book offer a range of four wheel drive adventures varying from delightful beginner jaunts to some very hard four wheeling. Don't overstep the boundaries imposed by your experience. If you are a beginner, enjoy the experience of learning the skills associated with four wheel driving slowly and easily. There will be plenty of time later to tackle the harder treks.

Just a word of WARNING here though. Tracks change. Rain, time and man can change a track significantly. The Department of Conservation and Natural Resources (Dept. of CNR) often have dozers working on our bush track network. What we might describe as a ''badly rutted track'' will be more like a well graded road if a Dept. of CNR dozer has been across it. Similarly, over time and with heavy rain, a track can go from a well graded road to being impassable. As well, a track you may find easy in the dry can become extremely dangerous in the wet.

Always drive with safety being the first criteria!

The Victorian Association of Four Wheel Drive Clubs (VAFWDC) has a drive training program, as do a number of individual clubs and commercial organisations. We heartily recommend any one of these to you.

As well, when you're in the bush be environmentally aware. ''Don't bugger the bush''. That way the delight and adventure you experience will be available for future four wheelers.

We hope you enjoy the treks in this book, we know we did.

Ron & Viv Moon
October 1993

# BIG DESERT ADVENTURE

Few tracks of any note cross the vastness of the Big Desert region of Victoria. While a number leave the main Murrayville-Yanac Road, only a couple are more than a short dead-end set of wheel marks put in for broombush harvesting or to a bee hive site.

In summer this area can be as harsh, dry and hot as any of Australia's more famous deserts. Winter, on the other hand, can bring cold weather, rain and the occasional flooded clay pan. Autumn and spring are the best times to visit, with spring bringing a wealth of wild flowers to colour the scene.

Animal life is scattered, but varied. Kangaroos can be seen browsing in the cleared areas, while rare birds such as the Mallee Fowl may be seen in the thick areas of scrub. In fact, the bird life of the desert is rich with parrots, finches, honeyeaters, pigeons, swallows and many others enlivening the scene. Reptiles, especially lizards are very common.

## STANDARD

Easy to medium. However, this country is remote with little traffic. Be completely self reliant. Carry water, adequate fuel, etc.

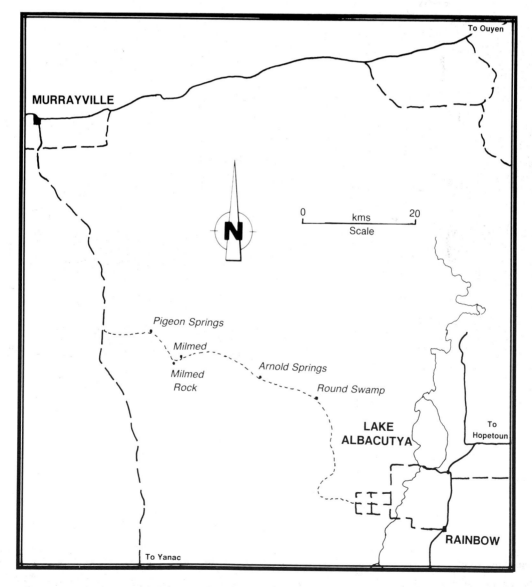

## DISTANCE and TIME

Murrayville, some 135 kms west of Ouyen and 460 kms (5–7 hours drive) north-west of Melbourne, lies in the heart of the mallee and is, in fact, much closer to Adelaide in South Australia, which is just 270 kms (4 hours drive) away. Rainbow, near the end of the trek, is 405 kms from Melbourne and 480 kms from Adelaide.

Total distance of this trek from Murrayville to Rainbow is around 146 kms, with driving time being 4–6 hours. However, it's really an excellent weekend jaunt.

## RECOMMENDED MAPS/GUIDES

No official maps show any tracks east of the Murrayville-Yanac Road. The best map, the 1:250,000 "Big Desert Adventurer" is not perfect, but is the best available. The 1:100,000 Auslig map "Albacutya" is handy for the southern section of the trek which shows "Round Swamp" as a 'waterhole' at GR 653481. Track information is accurate from this point, although all tracks used in this trek are not shown.

## CAMPING

There are a number of excellent campsites along this route, but you must take all your water with you.

## RESTRICTIONS

This area will soon be managed as a national park, so obey all requirements and signs. Stick to tracks, especially in the naturally cleared areas around springs and soaks.

Be extremely careful with fire.

The end of this trek passes through private farm land. Leave all gates as you find them and do not upset stock.

## TREK NOTES

**0.0 (0.0)**
Road junction — Ouyen Highway and turnoff to Nhill — on outskirts of Murrayville when heading east towards Ouyen — turn right. Signposted (SP) 'Nhill 150 km'.

**6.3 (6.3)**
Cross roads — proceed straight ahead (PSA) and road turns to dirt.

**10.0 (3.7)**
Cross roads — PSA. Road leaves farmlands and enters the desert country. Numerous tracks along this section — continue on main road.

**22.9 (12.9)**
Little Billy Bore and small cleared area on left — PSA.

**33.3 (10.4)**
Big Billy Bore and windmill on right — PSA. There is some pleasant camping amongst the trees with picnic tables and BBQ facilities.

**43.6 (10.3)**
Track on left — turn left. This track junction is marked by a blue metal triangle nailed to a small tree, as well as a small wooden signpost which reads 'Milmed Track'.
   Note: Straight ahead on the Nhill road 4.6 km further down the road you come to 'The Springs', a large cleared area with shade trees, picnic tables and BBQ facilities, making it a reasonable camping spot.

**54.6 (11.0)**
'Pigeon Springs' on right (SP). This large, cleared area offers some very good camping with plenty of large trees for shade.

**71.4 (16.8)**
Soak on left in amongst the bushes.

**72.2 (0.8)**
'Milmed Rock' on right — SP. A small, round outcrop of rock jutting upwards from the sandy desert floor. Visitors book located here.

**72.9 (0.7)**
Enter a large cleared area with some nice camping amongst reasonable size trees. The cleared area continues for another kilometre, offering plenty of opportunities for camping.

**73.0 (0.1)**
SP on left 'Milmed' — PSA.

**73.2 (0.2)**
Y-junction — veer left.

**80.1 (6.9)**
Spot Elevation Point — 500 metres to the right on top of sand hill.

**83.3 (3.2)**
Top of sandridge with great views overlooking a line of large sandridges to the right and down to the left to Arnold Springs.

**84.4 (1.1)**
'Arnold Springs' — SP on right — situated in a large cleared area, again with some pleasant camping and plenty of trees.

**92.0 (7.6)**
'Round Swamp' — SP on right — continue on main track which veers to the left, keeping the sign on your right. A faint track continues straight up the hill but is a dead-end track.
Round Swamp is situated in a large cleared area which offers some excellent camping amongst lots of large trees and pines. There is also a deep well, with shored sides, opposite the Round Swamp sign. Nearby is a small fenced area, like a grave site, that there is much conjecture about.

**92.9 (0.9)**
Old wooden channeling/fence — relics of the past, on the left.

**98.1 (5.2)**
Track on right — PSA. Righhand (RH) track SP 'Lookout 500 metres — Walkers Only'.

**103.1 (5.0)**
Track on left and fenceline — PSA following fenceline on your left. Also have farmland on your left along this section.

**104.0 (0.9)**
Spot elevation up on high point of sandridge to your right — 300 metres from track.

**104.2 (0.2)**
Faint track on right — PSA. At this junction the fenceline changes direction, swinging south-east.

**105.0 (0.8)**
Track on left — PSA on main track back into heath and mallee, leaving fenceline. Lefthand (LH) track follows fenceline.

**105.2 (0.2)**
Track on right — continue on main track which veers left. There are numerous tracks along this section — PSA on the main track.

**106.5 (1.3)**
Faint track on right — PSA. RH track goes up over the sandridge.

**107.6 (1.1)**
Y-junction — veer left. RH fork SP 'Hermies Garden No Through Road'.

**108.7 (1.1)**
Remains of old tank on right — PSA.

**109.5 (0.8)**
Track junction with fenceline and gate — turn right following fenceline on your left. SP on left 'Milmed Track'. A track continues straight ahead through the fenceline into farmland — do not use.
Numerous tracks coming in on the right along this section of track — PSA on main track which parallels the fenceline on the left.

**117.5 (8.0)**
T-junction — turn left, SP 'Pella Track'. Immediately after turning, pass through fenceline and gate and turn left again, following fenceline on your left.

**117.6 (0.1)**
Veer right away from the fenceline. Track proceeds through farmland.

**118.2 (0.6)**
Pass through fenceline and gate — PSA through farmland following fenceline on your right.

**119.1 (0.9)**
Pass through fenceline and gate, SP on right 'Chinaman's Well 12 km — Four Wheel Drive Only'.
Please leave all gates as you find them.

**121.1 (2.0)**
Major road junction — PSA passing farmhouse on right.

**122.1 (1.0)**
Cross roads — PSA. SP 'Pigick Pella Road'.

**124.1 (2.0)**
Cross roads — turn left.

**126.7 (2.6)**
Cross roads — turn right. Road you've been on was SP 'Schilling Rd'.

**128.7 (2.0)**
Cross roads — turn left. Road you've been on was SP 'Burma Rd'.

**131.2 (2.5)**
Y-junction — veer right and hit bitumen. SP 'Pigick-Kurmbrunin Rd/Kurmbrunin Rd'. LH fork is SP 'Bullygall Rd'.

**140.1 (8.9)**
Road on left — continue on main road which veers right. LH road is SP 'Westburn Beach Road' and 'Lake Albacutya Park'.

**140.4 (0.3)**
Cross bridge over Outlet Creek.

**146.0 (5.6)**
T-junction — LH leads to Hopetoun (40 km), RH leads to Rainbow.

# MT. BRIDE AND BRITANNIA CREEK

The forests of the Upper Yarra Valley are a real delight. South from Warburton is a large area of rugged forested mountains ideal for a number of day trips for four wheelers.

This trek takes you on a relatively easy run through the verdant greenery of the ranges, topping Mount Tugwell and Mount Bride in the process.

After following the crest of Britannia Range the route drops into the rich, dense fernery of Britannia Creek Road — one of the most picturesque strips of forest road around Melbourne.

While mountain and alpine ash dominate the higher peaks and ridges, on the lower slopes messmate, mountain grey gum and peppermint cover the hills. In the wetter areas huge tree ferns can be seen, along with smaller trees such as silver wattle, blackwood, sassafras and pomederris.

Before World War Two, timber tramways were about the only access to this region of Victoria. The bushfires of 1939 did an incredible amount of damage to the area and while today forestry is still carried on, the old sawmill sites are quiet, while the tramway lines make pleasant walking paths through the bush.

## STANDARD
Medium — if it's wet, some of the tracks can be interesting. If not, the route is fairly easy.

## DISTANCE and TIME
The trek starts 50 kms east of Melbourne at Wesburn, five kilometres before Warburton. Just over 31 kms later you are back on the highway. While the trek can be done in two to two and a half hours, take your time and enjoy the passing scenery.

## RECOMMENDED MAPS/GUIDES
Vicmap's 1:25,000 Gladysdale covers the area, although some tracks are not marked.

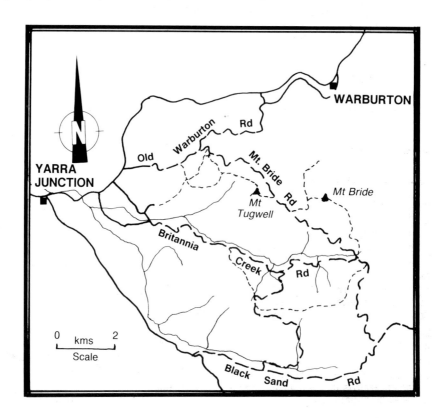

*Mount Bride Road beautiful easy climb thru rainforest*

# RESTRICTIONS/PERMITS REQUIRED

A number of tracks in this area are closed in winter, although generally this route remains open all year.

# TREK

**0.0 (0.0)**
Road junction of Warburton Highway and Old Warburton Road — road on right — turn right onto the Old Warburton Road.

**1.0 (1.0)**
Bitumen ends, road turns to dirt.

**1.1 (0.1)**
Major road junction — veer left following the Old Warburton Road.

**3.2 (2.1)**
Y-junction — veer right onto the Mount Bride Road. Old Warburton Road veers round to the left.

**3.8 (0.6)**
Track on right — turn right, signposted (SP) Edwardstown Road. Immediately after turning right you've got a track on the left — PSA on Edwardstown Road.

**5.5 (1.7)**
Large cleared logging area — turn left.

**5.6 (0.1)**
Y-junction — veer left.

**5.8 (0.2)**
Track veers around to the left and continues up the hill. Straight in front, before veering left, is a large fenced area.
   The track up the hill is deeply rutting and eroded, but not all that steep. However in wet conditions it would be extremely slippery.

**7.6 (1.8)**
Y-junction — veer left.

**8.2 (0.6)**
Good views to the left looking down into the valley.

**8.4 (0.2)**
Track on right — PSA.

**9.0 (0.6)**
Track on right — PSA, continuing on main track which veers round to the left along top of Mount Tugwell.

**9.1 (0.1)**
Track on left — PSA. There are numerous tracks along this section — continue on main track.

**9.6 (0.5)**
Major T-junction — turn right onto Mount Bride Road. SP Cemetery Track/Mount Bride Road.

**10.3 (0.7)**
Track on left — turn left, SP Burns Road.

**10.8 (0.5)**
Track on right — PSA on main track.
   There are numerous logging tracks in this area, continue on main track.

**11.1 (0.3)**
Y-junction — veer right, SP Mount Bride Track.

**11.8 (0.7)**
Faint track on left — veer right continuing on main track.
   This area has recently been logged, with numerous logging tracks off the main track — continue on the main track.

**12.1 (0.3)**
Track on left — PSA. Nice views along this section to the left overlooking the ranges.

**12.8 (0.7)**
Y-junction — veer right.

**13.6 (0.8)**
Track on right — continue on main track which veers round to the left.

**15.0 (1.4)**
T-junction — turn left onto Mount Bride Road and then just a short distance from this junction you have another track on your right — the Britannia Creek Road. Continue on the Mount Bride Road, which veers left at this junction.

**15.4 (0.4)**
Track on left — PSA. LH track SP Ezard Spur Road.

**15.6 (0.2)**
Track on right — turn right, SP Britannia Range Track.

**16.6 (1.0)**
Faint track on right — PSA.

**17.2 (0.6)**
Y-junction — veer right — at the top of the range in a cleared area. Disregard the faint track on your right which goes up the hill just before this junction.

**17.8 (0.6)**
Faint track on left — PSA. Immediately after this junction there is a track on your right — PSA.
   This area has been logged and there are numerous tracks in the area — continue on the main track.

**18.3 (0.5)**
Y-junction — veer left. RH fork is very faint.

**18.7 (0.4)**
Faint track on right — PSA.

**19.0 (0.3)**
T-junction — turn right.

**19.2 (0.2)**
Y-junction — veer left. Pass through some nice timber along this section.

**19.7 (0.5)**
Faint track on right — PSA.

13

**20.0 (0.3)**
Track on left — PSA.

**20.4 (0.4)**
Track on left — turn left. RH track leads to a deadend.

**20.6 (0.2)**
Track on left and immediately after you have a major T-junction — turn right, onto Portas Road.

**21.1 (0.5)**
Cross roads — PSA. RH track SP Britannia Range Track.

**21.5 (0.4)**
Sharp U-turn for the main Portas Road — Lady Walker Track off on left dropping off into thick scrub. Proceed on main Portas Road.

**23.2 (1.7)**
Track on right — PSA on main track.

**24.1 (0.9)**
Track junction with Britannia Creek Road — veer left onto Britannia Creek Road, paralleling Britannia Creek. This is a pleasant drive along this creek, with lots of tree ferns and some nice timber. Beautiful!

**25.5 (1.4)**
Track on right — PSA.

Just after track junction there is a log bridge across the creek.

**25.6 (0.1)**
Old sawmill site — worthwhile to stop and check the site out.

**26.2 (0.6)**
Track on left — PSA.

**27.0 (0.8)**
Track on right — PSA. RH track SP Justice Track.

**28.9 (1.9)**
Quarry on left and track dropping off steeply on the right — PSA on main track.

**29.1 (0.2)**
Y-junction — LH track SP Buffer Break Track — veer right.

**29.5 (0.4)**
T-junction — continue to follow Britannia Creek Road which goes around to the right and turns into bitumen.

**29.9 (0.4)**
T-junction — main road swings around to the left.

**31.2 (1.3)**
T-junction with Warburton Highway — turn left for Melbourne.

# BUTCHER COUNTRY AND THE MACALISTER RIVER

Magnificent Mt. Howitt, one of the highest mountains in Victoria, stands at the head of the Macalister River. Macalister springs, just 2 kms to the east of the peak, is a well known permanent source of water that not only succors thirsty bushwalkers, but also the river itself.

The river flows south, gaining rapidly in size and etching a deep, steep sided valley on its way through a wild and untamed stretch of Victoria's Alps.

This trek begins at Licola and heads north into the mountain vastness, firstly following the vibrant Wellington River and then crossing some of the best high plain region in the state. Bennison Plain, Dinner Plain, Lost Plain, Holmes Plain, Snowy Plain and more are crossed before the turnoff to Butcher Country is reached, just on the northern edge of Howitt Plain.

Such lush snow plain areas brought pioneer cattlemen into the region during the late 1860's and much of the Howitt Plain area was part of the famous Wonnangatta Station run. Mt. Skene, on the western side of the river, was part of cattle runs pioneered by cattlemen from Jamieson.

Once the Howitt Plains are left behind the route follows the Butcher Country Spur south. On the eastern side is the Caledonia River Valley, while on the other is the Macalister. There are some excellent views and some steep climbs before the final descent into the Macalister Valley.

For those who love bird life and who have a good eye, the variety of habitat along this trek results in a large number of species being observed. Robins, currawongs, pigeons, parrots, honeyeaters and birds of prey will be seen.

Flowers too are in rich array, especially in late spring and summer. The snow plains can be covered with everlasting daisies, while in the forested areas heaths, daisy bush, egg and bacon plants and orchids add their splash of colour.

The Macalister River acts as the boundary for the Alpine Park along much of this route. To the east is park and to the west other Conservation Forests & Lands managed land.

Deer shooting is poplar in this region and will continue on a seasonal basis.

## STANDARD
Medium to hard.

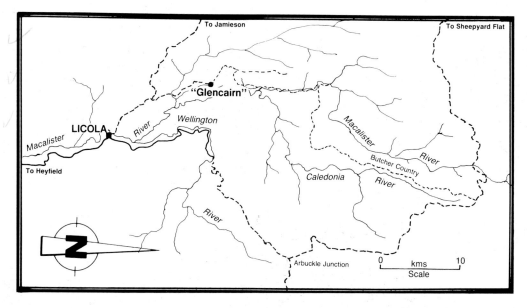

## DISTANCE and TIME

Licola, the beginning of this trek, is around 250 kms north-east of Melbourne and about 4 hours drive.

The round trip is about 150 kms and takes about 6–8 hrs driving, depending on how much trouble you have.

## RECOMMENDED MAPS/GUIDES

Macalister River Watershed (1:70,000) by S.R. & P.N. Brookes. Available in all good map stores in Melbourne, also Dargo and Licola general stores.

Other maps include AUSLIG 1:100,000 Maffra and Howitt or Div. of Survey and Mapping (Victoria) 1:50,000 Howitt-Selwyn (part only).

## CAMPING

There is some magnificent camping along this route. For starters there is camping along the Wellington River, up on the snow plains amongst the snow gums, or on numerous places along the Macalister River. A Conservation Forests & Lands designated camping area is to be established at the Junction of the Macalister and Calendonia Rivers.

## RESTRICTIONS/PERMITS REQUIRED

Part of the Alpine National Park, access restrictions apply over winter — normally from June to the end of October.

Carry out all rubbish. Leave camps clean and tidy.

Stick to marked tracks.

## TREK

**0.0 (0.0)**
Trek begins at the Y-junction just outside Licola, some 54 kms north of Heyfield — veer right for Butcher Country. Veer left across the bridge for Licola general store and camping ground just 300 meters away.

**11.0 (11.0)**
Enter Alpine National Park. First of a number of camping areas along the Wellington River on left.

**23.3 (12.3)**
Cross bridge and hit dirt road — proceed straight ahead (PSA). Camp site on right.

**37.8 (14.5)**
Track junction & Information Shelter on left — PSA. Area known as Tamboritha Saddle.

**48.3 (10.5)**
Y-junction — veer left. Arbuckle Junction.

**73.8 (25.5)**
Track on right — PSA. Righthand (RH) track is Zeka Spur Track which leads to Wonnangatta Valley.

**74.2 (0.4)**
Track on left — turn left. Signposted (SP) 'To Butcher Country'.

**74.3 (0.1)**
Fenceline and gate. Gate SP 'Road Closed until October 31st'. This track passes through quite a bit of flat area with lots of snow gums and some open valley/snow plain area.

**78.2 (3.9)**
Sign on left 'Moorooka National Park'.

**79.5 (1.3)**
Begin descent down the range.

**79.7 (0.2)**
Cleared area along the top of the ridge with good views to the right.

**81.0 (1.3)**
Good views travelling along the edge of the range. If you get out and just walk to the left a little, you'll get quite a view. Looks down into the headwaters of the Caledonia River.

**82.7 (1.7)**
Y-junction — veer left. Junction is just on top of a knoll.

**88.3 (5.6)**
Faint track on left — continue on main track round to right.

**94.4 (6.1)**
Very steep climb with some rocky steps to negotiate. Probably the hardest section of the trail, but there's been interesting sections before with more to come.

**96.5 (2.1)**
T-junction — turn left heading south.

**99.9 (3.4)**
T-junction — turn right.

**102.5 (2.6)**
Good views to the north as the track passes along the very edge of an escarpment.

**103.9 (1.4)**
Cross roads — PSA.

**104.0 (0.1)**
Track on left — continue on main track which veers to the right slightly.

**106.6 (2.6)**
Cross roads — turn left. The track straight ahead leads to a camp on the river. River now your right.

**107.1 (0.5)**
River crossing — take care. First crossing of the Macalister River. Can be a deep crossing, especially early in the season. Track you're on now is part of the National Horse Trail.

**107.6 (0.5)**
Track on left — PSA. Lefthand (LH) track leads to a small camp area on the river.

**108.3 (0.7)**
Track on right — veer left immediately into the river crossing. Take care. RH track leads to a number of small, nice camping areas just up from the river. Camping area amongst large gum trees right by the river. Some deep pools.

**108.8 (0.5)**
Camping area on right beside the river.

**110.1 (1.3)**
Track on right — PSA. RH track leads down to the river.

**110.9 (0.8)**
River Crossing — take care.

**111.0 (0.1)**
Track on right — PSA. Number of small camping areas here.

**111.4 (0.4)**
Large cleared area — good camping. River down to the left.

**111.5 (0.1)**
River Crossing — take care.

**113.5 (2.0)**
Track on right — PSA. RH track leads to a very small camping area and river.

**115.1 (1.6)**
River Crossing — take care.

**115.2 (0.1)**
River Crossing — take care.

**116.2 (1.0)**
River Crossing — take care.

**116.3 (0.1)**
Y-junction — veer right. LH track heads to the junction of the Caledonia River and the Macalister. Track that crosses the Macalister here is a deadend track, but after the river crossing it leads to a number of good camp sites along the Caledonia River

**119.7 (3.4)**
Track on left — continue on main track which veers round to the right.

**120.6 (0.9)**
Gate — PSA. Long climb up the range.

**122.9 (2.3)**
T-junction — turn left and pass through gate. Gate SP 'Road Closed until 31st October'. This is Bull Plain Spur track. Left leads to Licola, right to Merrijig.

**125.3 (2.4)**
Track on right — veer left.

**128.4 (3.1)**
Glencairn Station on left — PSA.

**134.8 (6.4)**
Barkly River bridge — PSA.

**138.9 (4.1)**
Y-junction — veer right.

**140.6 (1.7)**
Road junction with Jamieson-Heyfield Roads — turn left to Licola. Right leads to Jamieson.

**149.4 (8.8)**
Road junction — veer right to Licola.

**149.6 (0.2)**
Licola General Store and camping ground.

# TO COPPER CREEK AND WALHALLA

Walhalla was once a thriving gold mining town with a population of over 20,000 people. The valley rang to the clatter of the steam engines and the gold stamper and the surrounding hills and valleys were crisscrossed with small railways dragging in timber to feed the mines.

Situated in a steeply lined valley Walhalla nearly died when the gold ran out. While in recent years there has been some mining activity in the immediate area it is tourist the now keep the place alive.

Once you get to Walhalla there is plenty to amuse anyone. The Long Tunnel Mine, once the richest producer of gold in Victoria now has guided tours through it while there is plenty of attractions in and around the town to keep you busy. There is a pleasant camping area in the town and the place makes a good base to explore the nearby hills and valleys.

This trek starts at the Moondarra Reservoir which is well sign posted north of Moe. For much of its distance the trek follows the old stage coach road that once linked Walhalla with its port of Port Albert.

At the small hamlet of Copper Creek you'll find a few buildings and a small spot to camp beside the Thomson River.

Summer is a great time to visit the mountains and to enjoy the cool of the forest and the babbling streams. You can go bird watching or cast a line for a feed of trout.

## STANDARD
An easy to moderate trek that only has one sticky point and that is the crossing of the Thomson River. If the river is high it can be hairy. Even when it isn't there are a few rocks to get hung up on. Check the route across before plunging in. Even if you have crossed the river at this spot before it pays to check as any recent flood will change the crossing. You have been warned!

## DISTANCE AND TIME
The route from the reservoir to Walhalla is less than 30kms and takes about 2 hours at an enjoyable pace.

## RECOMMENDED MAPS/GUIDES
The best map for the trip is the Dept of CNR 1:100,000, Erica Operations Area map. This is only available from the CNR office at Erica. The other maps that cover this area and are a little easier to get are the Auslig 1:100,000 maps, Moe and Matlock.

## CAMPING
There are a couple of spots to camp at along this route the best spot being where the track crosses the Thomson River. You can also camp at a rather spectacular but exposed site at the Happy Go Lucky campground on the ridge above the Thompson or at Walhalla itself.

## RESTRICTIONS/PERMITS REQUIRED
The river is the only problem. No restrictions apply to this route as far as seasonal closures are concerned.

## TREK

The starting point for this trek is the Moondarra Reservoir, which is easily accessible from the township of Moe, itself about 136kms east of Melbourne. Head north from Moe towards Erica and follow the signs to the reservoir.

As you enter the small hamlet near the dam wall the trek begins at the 40 km/h sign which leads down to the dam wall.

**0.0 (0.0)**
Zero at the 40kph sign. Head down towards dam wall.

**0.5 (0.5)**
Dam wall - proceed straight ahead (PSA).

**0.7 (0.2)**
End of wall - turn right (TR).

**4.1 (3.4)**
Old track on right - PSA.

**4.8 (0.7)**
Track on right - PSA.

**4.9 (0.1)**
Track on right - PSA.

**5.5 (0.6)**
Track off to right - keep left.

**6.0 (0.5)**
Turn left (TL) sharply.

**6.1 (0.1)**
T-junction with bitumen road - TL.

**6.4 (0.3)**
Gravel road - PSA.

**12.4 (6.0)**
Road junction with sign post (SP) - PSA.

**12.5 (0.1)**
Bitumen road - PSA.

**14.4 (1.9)**
Road junction, SP 'Bluff Road' - PSA.

**15.2 (0.8)**
Cross roads - TR SP 'Copper Creek'.

**15.6 (0.4)**
Isolated but occupied houses - PSA.

**15.7 (0.1)**
Start winding, rocky and rutted descent PSA.

**17.8 (2.1)**
Copper Mine Hotel (private residence - keep out) - PSA.

**18.0 (0.2)**
Cross wooden bridge - PSA.

**18.1 (0.1)**
Y junction - veer right.

**18.3 (0.2)**
Thompson River crossing. The crossing is in two parts with a wide stone covered bar between the two. The second stretch of water is generally the deepest and there are a few large rocks to hang up the unwary. Be extremely careful if the water is deep. The force of the current can easily wash you downstream!

**18.4 (0.1)**
Tracks of to right and left - PSA uphill. This is a rocky, rutted climb.

**19.0 (0.6)**
Rebuilt road ledge on RH turn - PSA.

**22.1 (3.1)**
T junction - TL.

**23.1 (1.0)**
T junction - TL. Happy Go Lucky campground on right.

**24.4 (1.3)**
Road junction PSA.

**26.9 (2.5)**
T junction with bitumen road. Turn right (TR) to Walhalla or TL to Moe.

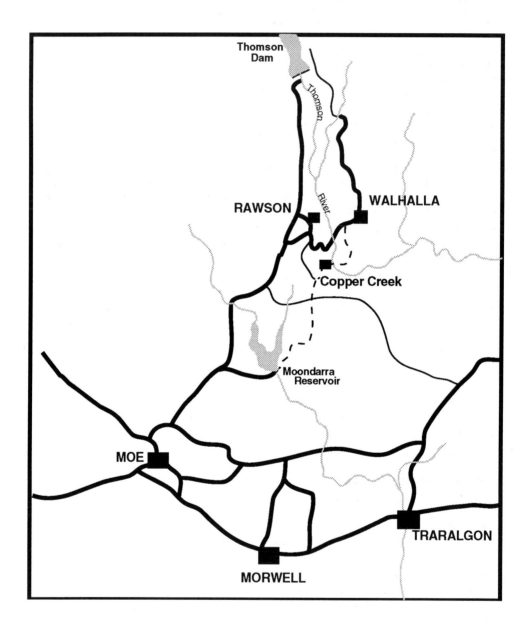

# THE CROOKED RIVER GOLDFIELDS

Angus McMillan was the first European into the rugged area behind the rich country of Gippsland. Blazing a way from the Monara in southern NSW, he reached Port Albert on the coast in 1839, and in that same year explored much of the hinterland.

While John Wilkinson, the government surveyor reported on the likelihood of gold during his work in the 1850's, it was Alfred Howitt who first reported good finds of the yellow metal. Commissioned by the government, Howitt left Melbourne in late May 1860. They found 'colour' in the upper Dargo, Wongungarra and Cooked Rivers before hitting a major find in Good Luck Creek, near its junction with Crooked River. News of the find leaked out at Christmas and within weeks there were over 700 diggers on the field. Bulltown, near the junction of Crooked River and Good Luck Creek, became the major town, but others sprang up down and upstream. Some semblance of permanence began to be established when reef gold was discovered in April 1864, and by June it was obvious that the town on top of the hill — Grant — was to outstrip the river-side towns in size and importance.

However, only two towns survived the turn of the century. Talbotville and Grant both endured. Grant was completely deserted by 1916, while Talbotville had one or two families there until 1950. Today the area is quiet and part of the Grant Historical Area and Alpine National Park.

This trek takes you from Dargo, via the High Plains Road to Grant Junction and onto Grant. It's worth some time to have a look around the old Grant township site. The cemetery, some street signs, the Jewellers Shop mine and the surrounding cleared area are not only interesting, but make some pleasant camp sites.

Good views can be had on the way to the top of Bulltown Spur and the descent is steep. Once on the river there are 30 river crossings before you end up heading back to Dargo, via the Crooked River Road.

Pleasant walks in the area can be had by following the river, the old bridle trails, or old mining races that criss cross the hill sides.

For those who want to try their luck, there is still gold being found in the creeks and rivers of the area. The camping is excellent, the bush peaceful and the scenery impressive.

## STANDARD
Easy to medium.

## DISTANCE and TIME
Dargo is some 300 kms east from Melbourne and 4–5 hours driving time.

Trek distance is about 70 kms, taking about 3 hours driving time.

Fill up with fuel and supplies at Dargo.

## RECOMMENDED MAPS/GUIDES
S.R. Brookes 1:70,000 Crooked River-Dargo.

## CAMPING
Excellent camping along the rivers or around the old Grant township site.

## RESTRICTIONS/PERMITS REQUIRED
As an Historic Reserve you're even allowed to take a dog into this section of the Alpine National Park. Shooting is also permitted — only of course with the normal licence and precautions.

To pan for gold you do need a Miners Right.

While access tracks in the area generally remain open all year, river heights can rise to dangerous levels, especially in the spring thaw. Be careful.

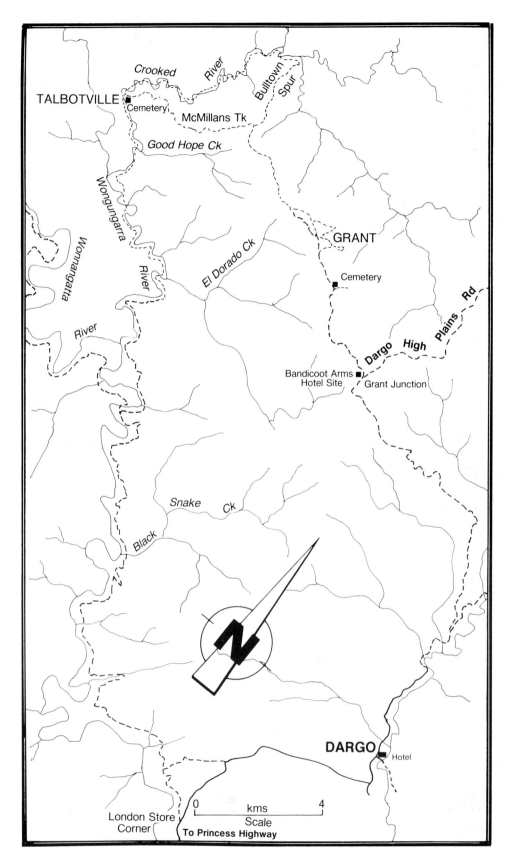

Crooked River

TALBOTVILLE
Cemetery

Bulltown Spur

McMillans Tk

Good Hope Ck

Wongungarra

River

Wonnangatta

River

El Dorado Ck

GRANT

Cemetery

River

Dargo High Plains Rd

Bandicoot Arms
Hotel Site

Grant Junction

Snake Ck

Black

DARGO
Hotel

0    kms    4
Scale

London Store
Corner

**To Princess Highway**

# TREK

**0.0 (0.0)**
Dargo — in front of the pub. Head north.

**5.0 (5.0)**
Y-junction — veer left.

**15.8 (10.8)**
Track on left — turn left. Grant Junction — signposted (SP) 'Grant/McMillans Track/Talbotville'.

**15.9 (0.1)**
Grant Historical area sign on left.

**19.3 (3.4)**
Track on right — proceed straight ahead (PSA). SP 'Jolly Sailor's'. Just past this track junction, on your right, you'll find the remains of a cemetery. There are a number of grave sites still discernible amongst the bush which is slowly engulfing it.

**20.7 (1.4)**
Y-junction — veer left. SP on tree 'Grant'.

**21.2 (0.5)**
T-junction — turn left. Numerous tracks around the junction, with the old town site of Grant being off to the right. It is well worth exploring this area and the old town site. Although there's not much left of what was once a thriving mining community, you'll still find a number of old mines, including the 'Jeweller's Shop' with it fern enshrouded entrance.

**22.5 (1.3)**
Helipad and good view to the right — PSA.

**22.8 (0.3)**
Y-junction — veer right. SP 'Collingwood Spur Track' (to left)/'McMillans Track — Talbotville' (to right).

**25.5 (2.7)**
Track on right — turn right. SP 'Bulltown Spur'. Steep descent.

**27.0 (1.5)**
Helipad with good views all round — PSA. Very steep descent.

**28.2 (1.2)**
Track on right — continue on main track which veers to left. Righthand (RH) track leads about 200 metres down to the river and a very pleasant, but small, camp site. Area around here was the site of Bulltown or Naarun.

**28.8 (0.6)**
First crossing of Crooked River. Just after crossing the river there are tracks both to the left and right which lead to a couple of good, large camp sites.

**28.9 (0.1)**
River crossing.

**29.4 (0.5)**
River crossing.

**29.7 (0.3)**
River crossing then track on right. RH track

leads to a nice, reasonably sized camp site in a cleared area. This area was the site of Hogtown.

**30.1 (0.4)**
Track on right — PSA. RH track leads to a reasonably large camp site.

**30.4 (0.3)**
River crossing.

**30.6 (0.2)**
Track on left — PSA. Lefthand (LH) track leads down to river.

**30.7 (0.1)**
River crossing.

**31.1 (0.4)**
River crossing.

**31.2 (0.1)**
River crossing then track on right. RH track leads to a very nice camp site, if just a bit close to the road.

**31.4 (0.2)**
River crossing.

**31.6 (0.2)**
River crossing.

**32.1 (0.5)**
River crossing.

**32.8 (0.7)**
River crossing then track on left. LH track leads to a small camp site.

**33.0 (0.2)**
First sighting of old mining hut stone ruins on right.

**33.1 (0.1)**
River crossing.

**33.2 (0.1)**
River crossing then track on left. LH track leads to small camping area. Stone hut ruins on right.

**33.4 (0.2)**
River crossing.

**33.9 (0.5)**
River crossing.

**34.1 (0.2)**
River crossing.

**34.3 (0.2)**
River crossing.

**34.7 (0.4)**
River crossing.

**35.0 (0.3)**
River crossing.

**35.1 (0.1)**
Faint track on left — PSA.

**35.2 (0.1)**
River crossing.

**35.3 (0.1)**
Track on right — PSA. SP 'Basalt Knob Track'.

**35.4 (0.1)**
River crossing.

**35.6 (0.2)**
River crossing.

**35.9 (0.3)**
River crossing and then enter a large cleared area which was the site of the township of Talbotville. There are a lot of camp sites around this clearing and alongside the river, with a number of large shade trees.

**36.0 (0.1)**
Track on left — PSA. SP 'McMillan's Track' — which leads up to the old cemetery, about 100 metres up, on your right.
   This area is accessible by 2WD (driven with care), with vehicles being able to gain access from Dargo via Grant Road and McMillan's Track, thus bypassing all of the river crossings.

**36.4 (0.4)**
River crossing.
   There are a number of alternative tracks crossing the river at this point. You can choose to either continue alongside the river for a short while or veer away to your right. All tracks join up towards to end of the cleared area.

**37.0 (0.6)**
Y-junction — veer right up and over a small rise. LH fork rejoins this track again in a short distance.

**37.8 (0.8)**
Enter large cleared area.

**37.9 (0.1)**
Gate/fenceline and river crossing. Large cleared area with possible camp sites down along the river.

**38.8 (0.9)**
Enter large cleared area.

**39.1 (0.3)**
Track junction — turn left continuing on main track. SP 'Crooked River Track'. Numerous tracks leading down to river.

**39.2 (0.1)**
Track on left — PSA. SP 'Collingwood Spur Track'.

**40.0 (0.8)**
Track on right — PSA. RH track leads down to a very nice camp site on the Wongungarra River.

**40.2 (0.2)**
Cross the Wongungarra River.

**41.3 (1.1)**
Y-junction — veer to left. RH fork is the main track. LH fork leads across nice river flats.

**42.6 (1.3)**
River crossing.

**43.0 (0.4)**
Small camping area. Track veers to the right and crosses the river and rejoins the main track which was left at the previous Y-junction. Turn left back onto the main track.

**44.2 (1.2)**
Track on right — PSA. SP 'Cynthia Spur Track'.

**44.3 (0.1)**
Camping area on left. Nice spot beside the river.

**44.4 (0.1)**
River crossing.

**44.6 (0.2)**
Track on left — PSA. SP 'Randall's Track'. Also track on right.

**45.0 (0.4)**
River crossing.

**45.1 (0.1)**
Fenceline and Gate.

**45.2 (0.1)**
River crossing.

**45.4 (0.2)**
Track on left — PSA. Private property on right.

**45.5 (0.1)**
House and farm buildings on right — PSA.

**47.0 (1.5)**
Old footbridge on right across river.

**47.9 (0.9)**
Fenceline and Gate.

**51.1 (3.2)**
Track on left — PSA. SP 'Conway's Track'.

**51.2 (0.1)**
T-junction — turn left. RH turn takes you over the Kingwell's Bridge and along the Wonnangatta Road.

**58.7 (7.5)**
Cross bridge and track on left — PSA. LH track leads along Black Snake Creek towards Kong Meng and Bootlace Mines and an old battery, but you'll need to do a bit of walking to reach the mines and old battery site.

**61.7 (3.0)**
Track on left — PSA. SP 'Maguire's Track'.

**71.1 (9.4)**
Y-junction — veer right. SP to 'Stratford'.

**73.3 (2.2)**
T-junction — at London Stores Corner — hit the bitumen. LH turn back to Dargo or RH turn over the bridge to Fernbank and the Princess Highway.
   Just over the bridge, on the right, is the Wonnangatta Caravan Park. It is situated in a picturesque park like setting alongside the Wonnangatta River. Facilities include a kiosk.

# EAST COAST JAUNT

This delightful trek beings in the small community of Cann River, in far east Gippsland. The route heads south towards the coast and then parallels it, sometimes in the Croajingolong National Park, at other times in the surrounding State Forest. The only places to camp are in the designated camping areas along the coast, established in the National Park.

The first areas where the coast can be met are at Thurra River and Point Hicks. Point Hicks is where Captain James Cook made his first sighting of the Australian mainland in 1770.

Croajingolong National Park itself is one of Australia's finest parks. Its inlets, sandy beaches, rocky cliffs, impressive sand dunes, magnificent coastal forest and heath lands, make it an idyllic place for camping and touring.

The variety of habitat, stretching from bare dunes to rich verdant forest, is a rich environment for many species of animals and birds. The forests in East Gippsland contain patches of temperate rainforest and a dense undergrowth of lilly pilly and sassafras. This trek takes you through forests of gigantic red bloodwoods, mahogany gums, yellow stringybarks, silver top ash and rough bark apple. Wildflowers and orchids bloom year round.

Much of the region was devastated in the 1983 fires and the regrowth in many areas is dense and impenetrable.

While the forests are home for a large group of animals, probably the most common one that tourers see are the black wallabies that skip across the road or down the verge. Bird life varies from small wrens and robins flitting through the bush, to pied oyster catchers, terns and gulls along the coast.

## STANDARD

This trek is easy to moderate. Only in the wet is it a medium trek when some of the trails can be a little slippery.

It is probably essential that you carry a saw with you when you do this trek as there is a lot of fallen timber across the tracks, especially early in the season.

## DISTANCE and TIME

The trek beings at Cann River, 452 kms (5 hours drive) east of Melbourne. Cann River to Mallacoota, via this trek is some 113 kms. You could easily do it in a day, especially if you are based at any one of the good camp sites along the way.

## RECOMMENDED MAPS/GUIDES

A number of maps cover this region. Probably the best one being the Conservation Forests and Lands 'Croajingolong National Parks and Approaches' map. While this map shows all the major routes, there are many tracks in the forest that aren't shown on the map. For more details the 1:100,000 AUSLIG series 'Cann and Mallacoota' cover this area.

## CAMPING

Designated camping areas at Thurra River, Mueller River Inlet, Wingan Inlet and Shipwreck Creek are managed by the CF&L. These areas are extremely popular at Christmas time and Easter and bookings need to be made during these peak periods through the CF&L. At other times of the year these camping areas are excellent places to stop for a day or week. Facilities offered vary, but camping areas have at least basic facilities.

Elsewhere in the park no other camping areas exist and the dense forest means that there are few opportunities to camp along the route.

## RESTRICTIONS/PERMITS REQUIRED

Parts of this trek are closed between 1st June to 30th September. Also, the bridge across the Wingan River is sometimes closed. Check with the CF&L office in Cann River to make sure that this track, the Wingan Link Road, is still open.

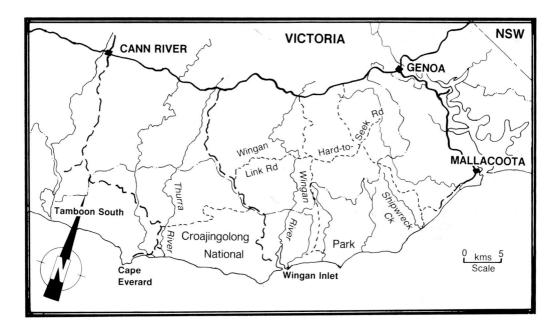

## TREK

### 0.0 (0.0)
Major cross roads — Princes
Highway/Cann Valley Highway, Cann River,
heading east (from Melbourne). Hotel on
left, service station and supermarket on
right. Turn right onto Tamboon Road,
signposted (SP) 'Tamboon Inlet/Point Hicks'.

### 7.5 (7.5)
Y-junction — veer left.

### 15.4 (7.9)
Y-junction — veer left onto the Point Hicks
Road towards Thurra River. Righthand (RH)
fork leads down to Cann River and Furnell.

### 20.4 (5.0)
Croajingolong National Park sign.

### 34.4 (14.0)
Track on left — turn left, SP 'Cicada
Trail/Mt. Everard Track'.

Continuing straight ahead leads to Mueller
River camping area and 5.4 kms from the
Cicada junction you cross the long wooden
bridge which spans the Thurra River. The
Thurra River camping area sites begin on
the other side of the bridge and the road
continues on a little further to Point Hicks.

The track into Mueller River camping area
is quite good, not very steep, giving good
access to Mueller River Inlet. Great
canoeing with close access to the inlet to
launch canoes. Camp sites 8–12 are drive-in
camp sites. With camp sites 1–6 it's
necessary to carry in all your gear from the
day visit area (cannot drive to the sites),
with No. 1 being the furthest one away
(about 100 yards walk) and almost on the
beach front, tucked in behind the sand
dunes. Good bird life and easy access to
the beach for walkers. No wood fires, gas
stoves only.

### 34.8 (0.4)
Y-junction — veer right, SP 'Road closed
1st June to 30th September'. Lefthand (LH)
fork SP 'Mt. Everard Track'. A little over 2
km and a walk of one kilometre will bring
you to the top of Mt. Everard. Good views.

### 35.8 (1.0)
Cross the Mueller River. The track along
this section passes through a dense
understorey of spindly wattle and low
bushes, with quite a few large banksias and
gums.

### 42.0 (6.2)
Walking track and car parking area on right,
SP 'All Day Track' — leads to beach near
Petrel Point. Continue on Cicada Track
which veers to the left.

### 46.8 (4.8)
Gus Track on left (SP) — PSA.

### 53.1 (6.3)
Cross Roads — PSA on Cicada Track.
Cross track SP 'Camp Creek Track'.

### 54.4 (1.3)
T-junction — turn left onto West Wingan
Road — a good, well maintained gravel
road. RH leads to Wingan Inlet (10.4 kms).
Pleasant camping amongst the trees by the
inlet, but there is about a 1/2 hour walk to
the beach. Boats can be launched in the
inlet, however there is 20hp limit on the
motor size. The water in the inlet is shallow
and the banks weedy.

### 61.8 (7.4)
Track on right — turn right, SP 'Wingan
Link Road'.

### 62.4 (0.6)
Track on right — PSA. RH track SP
'Surprise Creek Track' (fairly overgrown).

**63.5 (1.1)**
Track on left — PSA. LH track SP 'Wingan Link Shortcut'.

**73.6 (10.1)**
Cross Wingan River — bridged with gate. This gate can be shut, closing the bridge — check with Cann River Office before commencing trek.

**75.7 (2.1)**
T-junction — turn right onto East Wingan Road.

**75.9 (0.2)**
Track on left — PSA.

**76.3 (0.4)**
Track on right — PSA on Hard To Seek Track. RH track leads down to the river (3.5km from track junction) — bridge across river — no camp site.

**76.9 (0.6)**
Cross Hard To Seek Creek — bridged.

**78.5 (1.6)**
Faint track on right — PSA.

**79.5 (1.0)**
Track on right — PSA.

**80.5 (1.0)**
Track on right — PSA.

**82.4 (1.9)**
Cross cement causeway and rocky creek bed. This creek often runs fairly strongly — take care.

**83.0 (0.6)**
Track on right — PSA.

**85.2 (2.2)**
Track on left — continue on main track which veers right.

**85.3 (0.1)**
Cross roads — turn right onto Stony Peak Road.

**91.0 (5.7)**
Track on left — turn left onto Betka Track (SP).

**93.5 (2.5)**
Y-junction — continue on Betka Track which veers round to the right. LH fork SP 'Miners Track 4WD Only'.

**98.4 (4.9)**
Y-junction — veer right, SP 'Shipwreck Creek Camp'. LH track SP 'Aerodrome Track/Mallacoota 9km'.

**101.2 (2.8)**
Track on left — turn left onto Centre Track. Continuing straight ahead on Betka Track takes you down to Shipwreck Creek camping area (2.7 kms).

Shipwreck Creek camping area is situated amongst the forest with pit toilets and fire places. The camping area is not near the creek, and as such you would need to collect water from the creek further upstream when required. It's also a bit of a walk down to the beach.

**103.9 (2.7)**
Cross creek — bridged — track can be closed at this point.

**105.0 (1.1)**
Croajingolong National Park sign on right.

**105.5 (0.5)**
Y-junction — veer left.

**106.1 (0.6)**
Track on left — PSA on Centre Track/Shipwreck Creek Camp track (SP). LH track is SP 'Aerodrome Track'.

**107.0 (0.9)**
Track junction — PSA. Gun club on left — LH track leads to gun club.

**107.4 (0.4)**
Track on left — veer right continuing on main track.

**108.3 (0.9)**
T-junction — turn left. SP at junction 'Shipwreck Creek Camp'.

**108.8 (0.5)**
T-junction — turn left.

**110.6 (1.8)**
Cross Betka River — bridged and road turns to bitumen.

**113.2 (2.6)**
Mallacoota — roundabout in town centre. Mobile Service Station on left. Turn left for Genoa, or PSA for Mallacoota town centre.

# WHIPSTICK AND KAMAROOKA

The Whipstick and Kamarooka State Parks are located north of Bendigo and cover 2300ha and 6300ha respectively. While they are situated just a short distance apart, they are covered in different vegetation and have a completely different feel about them.

The Whipstick is dominated with an open forest of Red Ironbark, Yellow Gum and Grey Box, with large areas of Mallee scrub. Travellers will also pass through an area that is regularly harvested for eucalyptus oil distillation. Sunday travellers will have the opportunity to visit and tour an historic oil distillation plant, one of the few still operating in Victoria, along the route of this trek.

Kamarooka has much the same variety of vegetation with Yellow Gum and Grey Box forest, dotted though with Native Pine, Quandong and Desert Cassia. Large areas are also covered with a healthy cover of Mallee.

Gold was discovered in the Whipstick in 1857 and a few years later in the Kamarooka area, but it is the former which shows the most workings and relics from that rich past. Fossicking areas are still available in the Whipstick for those searching for a fortune and gold is still found.

Animal and bird life feature a good mix of the drier inland and the more temperate parts of Victoria.

Spring is without a doubt the best time to visit these areas. The wildflowers are delightful and make any trip worthwhile.

## STANDARD
This trek is easy to medium. If you strike rain the roads and tracks can be very slippery.

It is easy to get temporarily misplaced in the Whipstick and it has taken us ages to get to know this area well. The sheer number of tracks defy description and any map!

## DISTANCE AND TIME
Whipstick is located 160kms north of Melbourne, or less than 20kms north of Bendigo.

Elmore, where the trek ends is located on the Northern Highway, 160kms north of Melbourne and 76kms west of Shepparton.

The trek as detailed is just 76kms long and takes less than 3 hours. It is worth it to take your time, stop overnight in one of the camping areas you pass, go exploring or even fossicking.

## RECOMMENDED MAPS/GUIDES
There is not one good map or guide to this area. All the maps we know of show only the main routes with any degree of accuracy, while the many minor tracks are either not shown, or are so wrong they are useless.

The CNR map is probably the best as an overview. The Outdoor Press map 'Bendigo Goldfield-The Whipstick' is good for showing prospecting areas and the like for the Whipstick area only.

## CAMPING
There are a number of camping areas detailed in this trek. The sites in Kamarooka are our favourite as they have no facilities and no pine logs.

## RESTRICTIONS/PERMITS REQUIRED
Much work has been done on the tracks in both these parks. Please stick to the ones that are open and obey all the regulations.

## TREK

**0.0 (0.0)**
Main road junction on Loddon Valley Highway, in Eaglehawk, north of Bendigo, near library and townhall. Signposted (SP)
'Sailors Gully Rd. - Mitiamo/Whipstick Forest' - veer right.

**0.7 (0.7)**
Road on right - turn right (TR) - SP 'Whipstick Park - Leslie Rd.'

**1.2 (0.5)**
Road junction - veer half left up 'Whipstick Rd'.

**1.9 (0 .7)**
Bitumen ends and enter Eaglehawk Regional Park (SP).

**2,1 (0.2)**
Road junction - PSA. Track on right leads to Lightning Hill Lookout.

**2.2 (0.1)**
Track on left - turn left (TL) - SP 'Sandner Rd'.

**3.2 (1.0)**
Faint crossroads - proceed straight ahead (PSA).

**4.3 (1.1)**
Crossroads - PSA. Track on left leads to Sandner Picnic and camping area.

**4.9 (0.6)**
T-junction - TR.

**5.1 (0.2)**
Creek crossing. Beelzebub Gully - they don't come much bigger in the Whipstick.

**5.9 (0.8)**
Track junction - PSA onto better gravel road. Cleared farming land around here.

**6.5 (0.6)**
T-junction - TR.

**7.9 (1.4)**
Crossroads - PSA into forest.

**8.5 (0.6)**
Crossroads - TL.

**8.9 (0.4)**
Crossroads - PSA.

**9.8 (0.9)**
Dam on left - PSA.

**9.9 (0.1)**
T-junction - TL.

**10.0 (0.1)**
Track on left - TL onto Foxes Bend Rd (SP).

**10.1 (0.1)**
Large dam on left - possible camp site - PSA.

**11.2 (1.1)**
Crossroads - TR (track crosses channel).

**11.6 (0.4)**
Small cleared are on left beside channel, just after crossing - possible camp site - PSA.

**11.7 (0.1)**
Track comes in on left - continue on main track veering right.

**11.8 (0.1)**
Track on right - PSA.

**12.0 (0.2)**
Crossroads - TL onto main dirt road.

**12.4 (0.4)**
Y-junction - veer right.

**12.7 (0.3)**
Major crossroads - PSA crossing main road and then continuing on minor track veering slightly to the right. Track junction SP 'Whipstick State Park.

**12.8 (0.1)**
Veer right continuing up the hill, keeping the mine/rubbish dump on your left - the track is faint along this section and then skirts a dry creek bed on your left.

**13.2 (0.4)**
Veer left - track comes in on your right.

**13.8 (0.6)**
T-junction - TL.

**14.3 (0.5)**
T-junction - TL onto Elliot Road.

**15.4 (1.1)**
T-junction with main track - TR.

**15.7 (0.3)**
Track on right - PSA on Sandfly Road. Right hand (RH) track SP 'Miller Flat Road'.

**16.4 (0.7)**
Track on left - TL. SP 'Notley Picnic Area'.

**17.0 (0.6)**
Notley Picnic/Camping Area on right - PSA on Notley Road (SP).

This picnic area offers some pleasant camping in a large cleared area which is dotted with tall trees. A large dam is also located near the camping area. Facilities provided include pit toilets, tables and fire places.

**17.5 (0.5)**
T-junction - TR onto 'Nuggety Road' (SP). Left hand (LH) road is SP 'Rifle Range Road'.

**17.8 (0.3)**
T-junction - TL, continuing to follow the main road.

**19.4 (1.6)**
Track junction - turn hard right into 'Daly Road' (SP),

**20.9 (1.5)**
Crossroads - PSA onto good dirt road - Camp Road. Back into farmland and houses.

**21. 8 (0.9)**
Major T-junction - TL onto 'Neilborough Road' (SP). Junction SP LH 'Shadbolt Picnic Area, RH 'Eaglehawk'/'Notley Picnic Area'.

Also situated at the junction, on the LH corner, is the old Camp Hotel, which is now a private residence.

**22.0 (0.2)**
Y-junction - veer right onto 'Skylark Road'. Junction SP RH 'Skylark Road', LH 'Shadbolt Picnic Area'.

**22.7 (0.7)**
Pass Shadbolt Picnic Area - very pleasant place to stop with pit toilets, fireplaces and tables. You can also camp here and it is popular.

**23.3 (0.6)**
Track on left - TL. Continue along main track passing through some fairly dense, low vegetation. The track for the next 5kms is definitely 4WD and the vegetation becomes very dense.

**24.4 (1.1)**
Crossroads - TR. Continue following main track and through creek crossing.

**25.3 (0.9)**
Crossroads - PSA. The track continues east, passing through large areas of cleared scrub. The track becomes faint at times and can be confusing. The vegetation that has been left as a thin strip beside the track can be very dense and you'll definitely scratch the duco.

**26.5 (1.2)**
Crossroads - PSA. For the first 100 metres follow beside the track in the cleared area as the track itself is very overgrown. Drop back into the track when possible.

**27.7 (1.2)**
Track and old fenceline come in on the right - PSA along main track, keeping the fenceline on your right.

**28.2 (0.5)**
T-junction - TL onto major dirt road.

**28.4 (0.2)**
Y-junction - veer right onto Loeser Road (LH fork SP 'Black Rock Rd).

The Loeser Camping/Picnic Area is situated at this track junction and it is a reasonable camping area with fire places and picnic tables. There are no toilet facilities. An old boiler and ramshackle shed are located in the area, while a dam is situated nearby.

**31.3 (2.9)**
T-junction - TL onto the bitumen.

**31.7 (0.4)**
Hartlands Eucalyptus Distillery and Historic Farm on right - PSA - bitumen ends. Tours of the distillery are given on Sunday's only and eucalyptus oil is available for sale.

**36.8 (5.1)**
Track on left - PSA. LH track leads to the 'Whipstick Environment Centre'.

**39.6 (2.8)**
Crossroads - TR into forest, SP 'Kamarooka State Park' (no dogs), then veer left just inside the fence at the Y-junction. The RH fork is SP 'Dry Weather Road Only'.

**43.9 (4.3)**
Cleared area on right with large peppercorn tree - PSA on main track. This area would make a pleasant camping spot, however there are no facilities.

**44.1 (0.2)**
Rush Dam on right - PSA. A cleared area with a fire place is situated beside the dam, making a pleasant camp site.

**44.8 (0.7)**
Crossroads - PSA through gate and continue along 'Camp Rd'.

**47.3 (3.2)**
Y-junction - veer right.

**47.9 (0.6)**
Mulga Dam on left - fireplace and small camping area near dam. PSA.

**48.3 (0.4)**
Track junction - veer left. 'Harrower Rd'. comes in on right.

**48.8 (0.5)**
T-junction - TL onto bitumen and within 50metres TR onto 'Camp Rd'.

**49.2 (0.4)**
Y-junction - veer right.

**50.3 (1.1)**
Y-junction - veer left.

**50.6 (0.3)**
Crossroads - PSA.

**51. 8 (1.2)**
Y-junction - veer left. RH fork SP 'Clay Rd'.

**52.8 (1.0)**
Dam on left and campsite.

**53.0 (0.2)**
Track junction - TL.

**54.1 (1.1)**
Crossroads - PSA into Angle Rd.

**54.2 (0.1)**
Y-junction - veer right.

**54.9 (0.7)**
Dam on left and campsite.

**56.4 (1.5)**
Track junction - veer left, continuing on main track.

**57.0 (0.6)**
Dam and possible campsite on right.

**57.4 (0.4)**
Creek crossing - 'Mosquito Ck'.

**58.3 (0.9)**
T-junction - TR following fenceline.

**58.4 (0.1)**
Crossroads - TL passing through farmland.

**59.0 (0.6)**
Creek crossing - 'Round Ck'.

**59.3 (0.3)**
T-junction - TL onto good dirt road - 'Kellys Rd'.

**62.8 (3.5)**
Crossroads - TR for Elmore. Left leads to Raywood.

**76.1 (13.3)**
Elmore. TR for Melbourne, TL for Echuca.

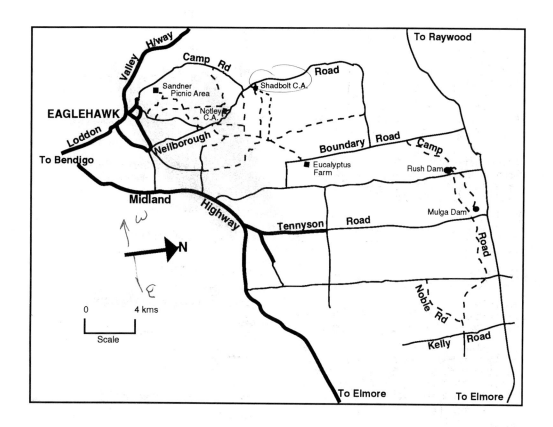

# ALONG THE HOWQUA

The Howqua River is one of the many delightful streams that cascade down from Victoria's high country. With its surround of high mountain peaks consisting of Mt. Howitt, Mt. Magdala, Mt. Lovick, The Bluff, Mt. Buller and Mt. Stirling, there are few other areas that can match it for visual splendour, verdant forests, cool mountain water and fabulous camping.

This trek takes you between Mt. Buller and Stirling, before dropping into the Howqua Valley, just above Bindaree Hut. From there the track skirts the river for a short distance before climbing towards the impressive bulk of The Bluff. Vegetation in this higher region changes to Alpine Ash and patches of Snow Gum, while on the craggy bluffs above, trees have disappeared to be replaced by snow plains. From these precipitous heights the route meanders back down into the Howqua Valley and the popular camping area around Sheepyard Flat.

There are a number of walks and short excursions to entice people out of their vehicles along this trek. Along Bindaree Road, before the Howqua is reached the first time, a short, pleasant walk can take you to the falls on Falls Creek. Longer walks can take you beside the river itself or even, for the fit and experienced, up to Mt. Howitt.

Fishing in the Howqua can be very rewarding, especially for those who expend a little effort getting to sections of the waterway that are rarely fished. The section between Pikes Flat and Bindaree Hut being reasonably productive and a half to full day's walk, depending on how much fishing you do.

This area, especially between Sheepyard Flat and 8 Mile Creek, is popular with deer hunters during the hunting season.

The weather can change dramatically in the course of a day, even in summer, and while sites along the rivers may be protected, the higher peaks can be encased in storms, fog and snow. Be prepared!

## STANDARD
Medium.

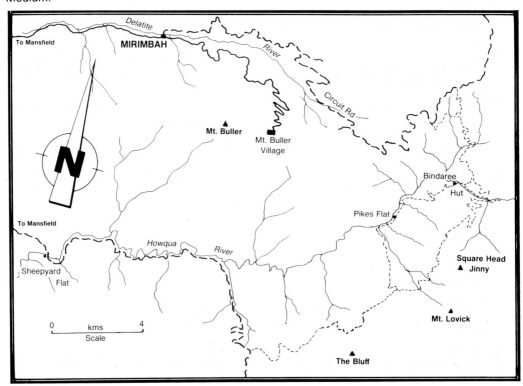

## DISTANCE and TIME

Merrijig, the beginning of the trek, is about 270 kms north-east of Melbourne, taking about 4–5 hours drive to get there from the centre of the city.

From Merrijig to the end of the trek is around 100 kms. Remember Merrijig has no fuel, so fill up at Mansfield or at Mirimbah, just before turning onto the dirt.

## RECOMMENDED MAPS/GUIDES

The 1:70,000 King, Howqua and Jamieson Rivers Map by S.R. & P.N. Brookes; the Vic Map 1:50,000 Howitt-Selwyn (part only), or the AUSLIG 1:100,000 Mansfield and Howitt maps.

## CAMPING

There are plenty of good sites along the river. Best spots include Bindaree Hut and Pikes Flat

## RESTRICTIONS

Part of the Alpine National Park and all regulations must be obeyed.

While access to near Bindaree Hut is possible all year by following the major Circuit and Bindaree Road, access is closed beyond the river crossing. Access is also available to the camping area near Sheepyard Flat all year, but you must come in from that end.

Take all rubbish out and do the right thing.

## TREK

**0.0 (0.0)**
Merrijig Pub — heading east towards Mirimbah and Mt. Stirling.

**13.2 (13.2)**
Road on left — turn left onto Stirling Road (towards Mt. Stirling) across the bridge. Road turns to gravel a short distance after.

**19.7 (6.5)**
Telephone Box Y-junction — veer right onto Circuit Road — Signposted (SP) 'Howqua Gap'.

**26.8 (7.1)**
Howqua Gap — proceed straight ahead (PSA) continuing along the main road.

**35.5 (8.7)**
Track on right — turn right off Circuit Road onto the track.

**37.2 (1.7)**
Cross Bindaree Creek.

**37.7 (0.5)**
T-junction — turn right onto the Bindaree Creek Road.

**38.7 (1.0)**
Track junction — veer right and keep on the main track.

**40.5 (1.8)**
Bridge across Falls Creek. Walking track on left up to the falls.

**42.5 (2.0)**
Track on right — turn right. Track heads steeply downhill to the Howqua River. Can be slippery!

**43.8 (1.3)**
T-junction — turn right for Bindaree Hut.

**44.0 (0.2)**
Cross Howqua River — PSA up the hill. Just over crossing on right is Bindaree Hut. Good camping along the river.

**44.1 (0.1)**
Track on left — keep right continuing on the main road.

**45.2 (1.1)**
Track junction — veer right.

**46.5 (1.3)**
Track on left — PSA.

**48.8 (2.3)**
Track on right — PSA. Righthand (RH) track leads down to the river and good camping spot.

**49.0 (0.2)**
Track on right — turn right down towards river into Pikes Flat.

**49.4 (0.4)**
Pikes Flat Hut. Good camping spot. Popular horse camp and fishing spot. Veer left, keeping the hut and fence on your right and begin to climb hill back up to main track.

**49.5 (0.1)**
Track junction — veer right, rejoining main track.

**49.6 (0.1)**
Gate.

**49.8 (0.2)**
Track on right — turn right.

**49.9 (0.1)**
Cross creek.

**50.0 (0.1)**
Track on left — PSA. Track begins to climb steeply and can be deeply eroded.

**50.4 (0.4)**
Cross 16 Mile Creek.

**50.5 (0.1)**
Track junction — turn left. Faint walking track veers right down to the river.

**51.5 (1.0)**
Cross creek — track begins to skirt 16 Mile Creek.

**54.1 (2.6)**
Track junction — turn right onto 16 Mile Road. Left leads back to the Howqua River, just above Bindaree Hut. Horse yards just before junction, dam and waterpoint near junction.

**54.8 (0.7)**
Track on left — PSA. Lefthand (LH) track SP 'Bluff Hut — 4x4 only'.

**59.3 (4.5)**
Parking area on left with Bluff Walking Trail leading straight up to the top of the Bluff — PSA.

**65.0 (5.7)**
Major track junction — turn right for

Sheepyard Flat and Merrijig. SP 'Bluff Link Road/Brocks Road'.

**81.8 (16.8)**
Tunnel Spur Flat Camping Area on the right.

**82.8 (1.0)**
Pickerings Flat camping area on right.

**83.4 (0.6)**
Davids Flat camping area on right.

**83.8 (0.4)**
Sheepyard Flat — plenty of flat area for camping with toilet facilities, complete with log fences. 2WD access.

**84.0 (0.2)**
Cross Howqua River and continue following major dirt road.

**100.3 (16.3)**
Road junction — turn left onto main bitumen road just a few kilometres east of Merrijig.

**102.4 (2.1)**
Merrijig Hunt Club Hotel on left.

# LERDERDERG

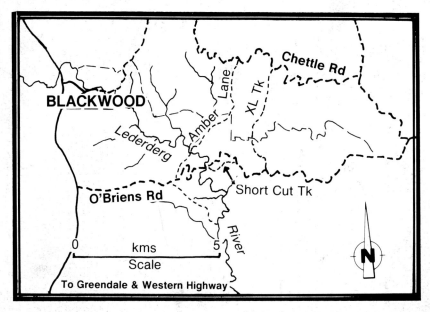

Lerderderg Gorge State Park lies to the west of Melbourne and this trek is, under dry conditions, an easy day's run from the city.

However, the area does offer some fine camping and is definitely worth more than a quick day trip. While there are a number of pleasant camp sites mentioned in the text, there are also some very good camping grounds in at Blackwood township.

Blackwood itself nestles in amongst the hills of the Upper Lerderderg River and owes its existence to the discovery of gold there in 1854. Within a year Blackwood was flourishing and soon had 13,000 people in and around it, with smaller townships at Golden Point, Red Hill and Simmon's Reef.

Today all the mines are closed, abandoned, with most lost in the bush. Blackwood is small and quiet, nestling around the pub and the general store that make up the centre of town.

Nearby the Blackwood Mineral Springs Caravan Park (for bookings phone the Ranger (053) 68 6539) cater for the small, but steady number of holiday makers that come here to escape the pressures of city life.

Located in the middle of Victoria's mineral springs region, the park has two springs that continually flow and these attract many visitors wanting to sample this sparkling bounty.

Throughout the forest messmate and stringybarks dominate the scene, while many other smaller wattles and shrubs vie for a position. Wild flowers, especially pink heath, often put on a spectacular display that changes the sea of drab green to one of colour.

Animal life is never startling, but for the observant and the lucky ones Koalas, Grey Kangaroos and Swamp Wallabies can be seen, along with a good range of birds.

## STANDARD
This trek is moderate to hard in the dry. When it's wet it's definitely hard.

## DISTANCE and TIME
Greendale and Blackwood are situated less than 100 kms west of Melbourne, taking just over an hour to get there.

The trek as detailed is just 37 kms and can take from 2 hours to 5 or 6 (or more) de on the weather and track conditions. It starts at the small town of Greendale, just the Western Highway and ends at Blackwood.

## RECOMMENDED MAPS/GUIDES

The Conservation Forests & Lands map on Lerderderg Gorge is probably the best map of the region. They are available from Conservation Forests & Lands or from good map shops such as Bowyangs.

## CAMPING

Generally wherever a track crosses a river or creek there is some pleasant camping. O'Briens Crossing is a nice spot, but popular — better to go somewhere else unless you're there mid week and no one else is.

## RESTRICTIONS/PERMITS REQUIRED

Some of these tracks get closed off during the wetter months. Please obey the regulations.

# TREK

**0.0 (0.0)**
T-junction in Greendale township (Hotel on right) — turn right. Signposted (SP) (to left) 'Ballan', (to right) 'Blackwood/Blackwood Mineral Springs'.

**2.3 (2.3)**
Wombat State Forest sign on left — proceed straight ahead (PSA).

**5.8 (3.5)**
Lerderderg State Park sign on right — PSA.

**7.1 (1.3)**
Road on right — turn right, now on dirt. Righthand (RH) road is O'Brien Road.

**7.6 (0.5)**
Track on left — PSA. Lefthand (LH) track is Kangaroo Track.

**9.4 (1.8)**
Track on left — PSA.

**10.4 (1.0)**
Track on right — PSA. RH track is Nolan Track.

**10.5 (0.1)**
Track on left — PSA. LH track is Ambler Lane Track.

**13.0 (2.5)** *Bridge. Very pretty*
O'Brien's Crossing over the Lerderderg *go +e* River. There are a number of walking tracks around this area.

**13.4 (0.4)**
Track on right — turn right up the hill (short cut track). It's a steep and a difficult climb — definitely a 4WD track. *CLOSED*
*PSA for 2.0 to T J*

**14.6 (1.2)**
T-junction — turn right, rejoining the main *dirt* track.

**15.0 (0.4)** *CLOSED*
Track on left — continue on main track which veers round to the right. LH track is Trout Track.

**15.2 (0.2)**
Track on right — PSA. RH track is Cowan Track, also dam on right — sign advising seasonal road closure.

**15.3 (0.1)** *go up here! excellent. trail in*
Track on right — continue on main track which veers round to left. *30. wood sl*

**15.9 (0.6)**
Track on left — PSA. LH track is on sharp curve in the road.

**16.1 (0.2)** *open*
Track on left — turn left. LH track is XL Track, SP '4WD Track Only'. Dam on right. Just after turning left a track comes in on left — PSA.

**17.5 (1.4)**
Sardine Creek crossing. Nice camping and picnic spot. Entry to creek severely chopped up. Quite steep and eroded track, with deep ruts up the hill after the creek crossing. *yes! 1 + deep* Difficult in dry conditions, extremely hard when wet.

**19.1 (1.6)** *1.7 – 1.8 ?*
Track on right — PSA.

**20.4 (1.3)** *0.3*
Track on left — PSA.

**21.0 (0.6)**
Cross roads — hit the main track — turn left.

**22.1 (1.1)** *steep begining. Can't get up → ridge rd. fast smooth*
Track on right — PSA.

**23.5 (1.4)**
Cross roads — turn left onto Amblers Lane. Track you've just come off is Chettle Road.

**24.1 (0.6)**
Faint track on right — PSA.

**25.6 (1.2)**
Faint cross road — PSA. SP 'Lerderderg State Park'.

**27.6 (2.0)**
Faint track on right — continue on main track which veers round to left. RH track leads into a nice camping spot on the river.

**27.7 (0.1)** *2 deep*
Cross Lerderderg River and track on right — continue on main track which veers round to left. RH track leads to camp sites. *there* From the river crossing the track is quite steep and difficult when wet. *f+wide*

**29.4 (1.7)**
Major T-junction with O'Brien Road — turn right.

**32.8 (3.4)**
T-junction — hit bitumen road — turn right to Blackwood, or left returns you to Greendale and Melbourne.

**36.4 (3.6)**
Y-junction — veer right to Blackwood. Left leads to Tretham.

**36.6 (0.2)**
Blackwood Hotel.

# MT. WELLINGTON, MILLERS HUT AND BILLY GOAT BLUFF

From Licola to Dargo is some of the finest mountain country in Victoria. This trek takes you into Millers Hut, via Mount Wellington, where one of the finest vistas in the Alps can be experienced.

Pioneered by Malcolm Macfarlane in the mid 1840's, the Mt. Wellington region was part of the Glenfalloch B Station situated on the Macalister River, south of present day Licola.

Lake Tarli Karng, a hidden mountain tarn, was discovered by a local cattleman in 1886 and subsequently visited by the explorer Dr. Alfred Howitt in 1887. Tarli Karng is the only natural lake in the Victorian Alps and has long been a popular destination for bushwalkers. Millers Hut is the closest vehicle access and the walk to the lake is steep, but very worthwhile.

The Wellington River, followed for much of the route north of Licola, starts its journey to the sea in a small way 150 metres below the lake. The lake itself has no natural outlet and water seeping through the barriers of rock and earth spawns the Wellington.

On the way into Millers Hut an infant Moroka River is crossed and once again on the way to Eastern Pinnacle it is crossed at Moroka Bridge.

The views from the Pinnacle fire lookout are also impressive and it's no wonder that a Conservation Forests & Lands ranger lives there during the summer season.

Billy Goat Bluff Track begins its descent in spectacular fashion and is steep all the way to the Wonnangatta Valley Road. From here to Dargo it is a pleasant run through alternating forest and grazing land.

## STANDARD
Easy to medium. If the snow plain areas on the way to Millers Hut are wet they can be extremely boggy. It's best to give it a miss at these times for environmental and mechanical reasons!

## DISTANCE and TIME
Licola is some 250 kms east from Melbourne and about 4 hours drive.

From Licola to the Mt. Wellington turnoff allow one to one and a half hours.

From the turnoff to Millers Hut — one hour each way.

From the turnoff to East Pinnacle — half an hour.

From East Pinnacle to Dargo — one to one and a half hours.

Total distance is 162 kms.

## RECOMMENDED MAPS/GUIDES
1:70,000 Crooked River/Dargo and Macalister River Watershed map by S.R. & P.N. Brookes. AUSLIG 1:100,000 maps Howitt, Dargo, Maffra and Stratford.

## CAMPING
There are a number of sites to camp along the way, generally along the Wellington River and at the Moroka Bridge crossing. Millers Hut is an ideal place to camp amongst magnificent, gnarled snow gums, but take water with you.

## RESTRICTIONS/PERMITS REQUIRED
Most of this trek is in the Alpine National Park and all regulations (e.g. no dogs, rifles, etc.) must be obeyed.

During winter the tracks to Millers Hut and Billy Goat Bluff are closed.

Please observe any fire restrictions and carry out all rubbish.

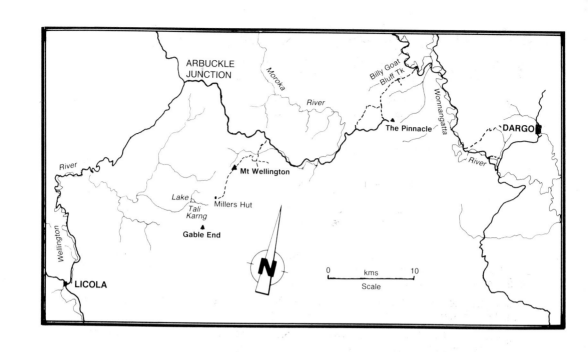

ARBUCKLE
JUNCTION

Moroka

River

Billy Goat
Bluff Tk

Wonnangatta

The Pinnacle

DARGO

River

Mt Wellington

Lake
Tali
Karng

Millers Hut

Gable End

N

LICOLA

Wellington

River

River

0        kms        10
Scale

# TREK

**0.0 (0.0)**
Road junction just outside Licola. No camping along the Wellington River within 10 kms of Licola. About 11 kms out the first camp sites are off to your left, just after you pass the Alpine National Park sign. About sixteen and a half kms out you cross the Wellington River and a number of camp sites around there, one off to the right just after you cross the river. Bitumen road still continues, so it's all 2WD access. Less campsites after the bridge.

A couple more bridges across the river give opportunities to get down onto the river for camp sites. Road then leads into the mountains.

**22.7 (22.7)**
Track on left — proceed straight ahead (PSA), signposted (SP) 'Fireplace'. Looks like the track leads down to the far side of the river to numerous camp sites. Also a number of camp spots to the left along the river just after the track junction.

**23.3 (0.6)**
Cross last of bridges and hit dirt road — PSA. Camp sites on right, immediately after crossing the bridge, alongside the river (2WD access).

**37.8 (14.5)**
Track and Information Shelter on left — Tamboritha Saddle — PSA. Cattle yards also on left.

**45.8 (8.0)**
Enter 'The Lost Plain' area — SP on left — PSA.

**48.3 (2.5)**
Y-junction (Arbuckle Junction) — veer right. Lefthand (LH) fork leads to Butcher Country and Mt. Howitt.

**51.1 (2.8)**
Track on left into Surveyors Creek Camp — PSA.

**52.4 (1.3)**
Track on left — PSA. LH track is the Moroka Glen Track.

**60.8 (8.4)**
McFarlane Saddle and track on right — PSA. Righthand (RH) track leads to the car park and walking track to Tarli Karng.

**66.2 (5.4)**
Track on right — PSA. RH track leads to Mt. Wellington and Miller's Hut.

### TRACK INTO MT. WELLINGTON AND MILLER'S HUT

**0.0 (0.0)**
Track junction into Miller's Hut/Mt. Wellington

**2.3 (2.3)**
Cross Moroka River.

**3.4 (1.1)**
Gate and Y-junction — veer sharp right, SP to 'Mt. Wellington', then almost immediately after turning go through another gate. Hard LH track is SP 'Moroka Range Track'. Track straight ahead is SP 'Avon Wilderness'.

**7.7 (4.3)**
Cairn on top of Mt. Wellington (1635 m). Track up is reasonably steep and rocky in places, but is well worth the effort as you've got the best views you could get of Victoria's high country. A magnificent 360° view of endless mountain ranges and snow plains, leading down into the valleys and plains below.

For the next few kilometres you traverse the ridge line of Mt. Wellington. There are quite a few sections that would be very boggy in wet conditions.

The last couple of kilometres down into Miller's Hut is quite a steep descent, eroded and rocky — slow going.

**12.6 (4.9)**
T-junction — turn left. RH track is SP 'Closed'.

**12.7 (0.1)**
Miller's Hut. The hut is surrounded by quite a large cleared area of land, making a nice spot to camp. No water though.

**67.2 (1.0)**
Old hut ruins on left — PSA.

**75.4 (8.2)**
Enter large cleared area with nice camping on left and cross bridge over Moroka River.

Tracks on right (after bridge) — PSA, SP on left 'Billy Goat Bluff Track'. Hard RH track leads down to the Moroka River and some nice camping sites — 2WD access. RH track, SP '4WD/Valencia Creek/Briagalong'.

**77.8 (2.4)**
Track on right — PSA, SP 'Logging Road Only — No Through Road for 2WD Vehicles'. This is the limit of 2WDs. RH track SP 'Marathon Road/Briagalong'.

**79.8 (2.0)**
Track on left — PSA. LH track SP 'Horseyard Flat'.

**83.9 (4.1)**
Y-junction — veer right, SP 'Pinnacles/Billy Goat Bluff Track'. Old Forestry sign reads 'Little Round Plain logging area. Project commenced 1966. Regeneration by autumn burning and aerial seeding at 2 lb Alpine Ash seed an acre. Forest Commission.'

**85.2 (1.3)**
Track on right — PSA.

**87.8 (2.6)**
Y-junction — veer left, SP 'Billy Goat Bluff Track'. RH track SP 'Pinnacles'.

### TREK UP TO THE FIRE LOOKOUT AT EAST PINNACLE

**0.0 (0.0)**
Y-junction — veer right.

**0.8 (0.8)**
Faint track on left — PSA. LH track SP 'Road Closed'.

**1.4 (0.6)**
Track on right — PSA. RH track SP 'Castlehill Track'.

**1.8 (0.4)**
Bottom of the steps leading up to the fire lookout on the East Pinnacle (1460 m). Short, but steep climb, up the steps to the fire lookout, but well worth the effort. Great views of surrounding ranges across to the Wonnangatta-Moroka National Park and the Wonnangatta River valley.

**89.0 (1.2)**
Y-junction — veer right, SP 'Billy Goat Bluff'.

**90.0 (1.0)**
T-junction — turn right, SP 'Billy Goat Bluff'. Track travels along the very top of the ridge line with some very impressive views.
 The track for the next 4.5 kms, although steep in parts, is good.

**94.5 (4.5)**
Helipad. The track veers to the right on the top of the helipad and continues to descend. SP on right 'Alpine National Park'.
 The track for next few kilometres is steep in sections, but good.

**97.7 (3.2)**
T-junction — turn right for Dargo. Left leads to Wonnangatta.

**103.6 (5.9)**
Kingwell's Bridge — PSA. Immediately after bridge is track on left — Conway's Track, leading to Crooked River.

**124.9 (21.3)**
Road on left — turn left to Dargo on Short Cut Road. Straight ahead leads to the Princess Highway.

**127.1 (2.2)**
Major road junction — veer left onto bitumen towards Dargo. Right leads to the Princess Highway and Bairnsdale.

**133.2 (6.1)**
Dargo Pub.

# LITTLE DESERT NATIONAL PARK

The Little Desert is situated between the South Australian/Victorian border in the west, and the township of Dimboola in the east. Covering 130,000 hectares, all the crown land within the region was incorporated into the Little Desert National Park in 1986.

Divided into three major blocks, it is the Eastern Block between Dimboola and the Goroke-Nhill Road which incorporates a stretch of the Wimmera River, that is the most popular. The Central Block and the Western Block are correspondingly less used, to the stage that the area around the border hardly sees anyone at all. Such remoteness is unique in Victoria.

While some of the tracks through the park, such as Stans Camp Track, date back to the 1850's, most of them date to the time when the area was about to be subdivided for farming. As late as 1969 much of the region was to be part of a government sponsored land development scheme. Thankfully conservationists (mainly the Victorian National Parks Association) stopped the subdivision and the region is now available for the public to enjoy.

Signs of early European attempts to use this region range from broken fence lines, dams, old windmills such as Dahlenburgs Mill, and hut sites such as McCabes Hut. Life for those pioneers was difficult. Could you imagine trying to raise sheep in this country? The water supply was low and erratic and the sandy soils very infertile. Apart from some sheep grazing and the seasonal honey collectors, there has been little agriculture carried out here.

Aborigines generally stayed away from this area, preferring the better country to the south and east. There have been a few transient camps found along the Wimmera River where mill stones, ochre, spearpoints and axeheads have been found.

The sandy nature of the land supports mainly mallee and heathland. Mallee, and there are a number of species, usually occurs with a scattering of other trees such as grey mulga and wattle, as well as shrubs such as hopbush, desert cassia and emu bush.

The heathlands found throughout the Little Desert have a great diversity of plants which produce a spectacular exhibition of wildflowers, especially in spring. Desert banksia, she-oaks, broom bush, several backias, corria, velvet bush, holly grevillea, as well as brush and flame heath are just some that account for the brilliant displays.

Larger trees such as yellow gums occur where clay soils are present near the surface; brown stringybark occurs widely, often amongst the heaths, while red gums and black box are found along the Wimmera River and in the infrequent swampy areas.

Birds are common in the park, especially parrots, along with many species of honeyeaters, babblers, finches and the occasional bird of prey.

One of the main reasons for the park is the existence of the Mallee Fowl. This industrious bird, about the size of a turkey, builds a large incubating mound to lay its eggs in. While they are present throughout the desert, probably the best place to see them is at the Little Desert Lodge (accommodation and camping also available) just north of the park on the Goroke-Nhill Road.

Now and then Kangaroos, possums and bats can also be seen, along with a good variety of lizards and the occasional snake.

## STANDARD
Easy, but remote. After rain some of the regions become boggy, particularly around clay pans.

## DISTANCE and TIME
Goroke is 375 kms west of Melbourne and about 5 hours drive.

The route described in the trek is a pleasant day's run. A weekend or more could be spent in the region, especially during early spring.

## RECOMMENDED MAPS/GUIDES
The best map is the Algona 'Little Desert National Park' available in good map stores such as Bowyangs (Kew) and the Melbourne Map Centre.

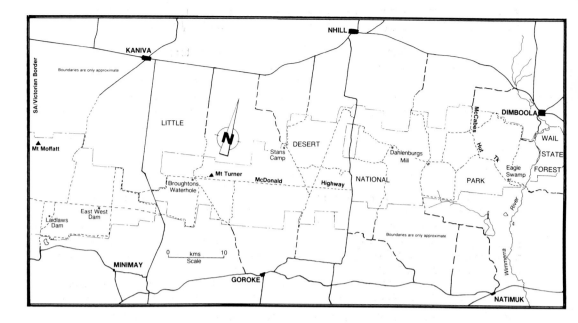

## CAMPING

A number of areas have been mentioned in the trek notes. There are a number of other established camping areas within the park which are maintained by the National Parks and Wildlife Service.

This trek beings 21 kms west of Goroke, on the Edenhope-Kaniva Road, and ends at Pimpinio on the Western Highway, south of Dimboola.

## RESTRICTIONS/PERMITS REQUIRED

None on the route described. Don't forget the park is surrounded by private land. Don't go off the tracks within the park and obey any signs and National Parks and Wildlife Service requirements. Carry water at all times. The temperatures during summer can be extremely high.

## TREK

**0.0 (0.0)**
Major Cross Roads 21km west of Goroke. Proceed north to Kaniva on Edenhope Road. (West leads to Francis).

**3.1 (3.1)**
Road on left — turn left. (Pass swamp area on right just after turning).

**8.7 (5.6)**
Y-Junction — veer right and proceed through Minimay township.

**23.5 (14.8)**
Sweeping Y-junction and then main T-junction — turn right. (Signposted to the left 9.5 to Francis).

**24.1 (0.6)**
Pass through Tallagerra. A very impressive and large homestead.

**24.8 (0.7)**
Continue on main road round to the left. Track degenerates quickly once you start hitting the sand area.

**27.5 (2.7)**
Track junction — veer slightly right — Signposted (SP) 'Laidlaws Dam Track'. The main road continues straight ahead, while the track hard right runs along the fence line.

**28.0 (0.5)**
Car bodies on left in cleared area.

**30.4 (2.4)**
Laidlaws Dam on left (SP). This section of track could become quite boggy when wet.

**33.2 (2.8)**
Cross Roads — turn right onto East West Track. A very faint track continues straight ahead.

**34.8 (1.6)**
Track on right — PSA. Righthand (RH) track is Neuarpurr Track.

**35.7 (0.9)**
Track on left — PSA. Lefthand (LH) track is Central Track. This section of track would be extremely boggy when wet.

**38.4 (2.7)**
East West Dam on right with good camping by the dam.

**41.3 (2.9)**
Cross Roads — turn left onto Jacobs Track, leaving the well used East West Track behind.

**43.7 (2.4)**
Faint track on right — PSA. RH track leads to water point.

**48.1 (4.4)**
T-junction — turn right onto Elliots track.

**51.1 (3.0)**
Hit a fence line (private farmland ahead) — turn right, following the track with fence line on your left.

**52.8 (1.7)**
Faint track on right — PSA. RH track leads to water point.

**53.9 (1.1)**
Faint track on right — PSA. RH track leads to water point.

**54.5 (0.6)**
T-junction — turn left continuing on main track with fence line still on your left. Faint RH track leads to water point.

**57.6 (3.1)**
Track on right — PSA on Spriggs Lane following the fence line on your left. RH track is continuation of the Northern Boundary Track around the Park.

**58.1 (0.5)**
Pass across a swamp area between two dams and follow fence line around to left. Beware if there has been any rain — it could be extremely wet and boggy.
  Cut across to the main bitumen road when possible.

**60.3 (2.2)**
Hit main bitumen road — turn right onto the Edenhope Road.

**61.0 (0.7)**
Faint track on left — turn left. Keep a good lookout for this track as it is easily missed. Track is on edge of farmland and follows along fence line on your left.

**63.7 (2.7)**
Track follows fenceline around to left.

**64.1 (0.4)**
Track goes around to the right continuing to follow fence line.

**64.8 (0.7)**
Track goes round to the left following the fence line.

**65.9 (1.1)**
Track on left — PSA. LH track continues to follow fence line.

**67.1 (1.2)**
Cross Roads — turn right onto McDonald Highway. A faint track continues straight ahead.

**69.2 (2.1)**
Track on left — PSA. LH track is Plains Track.

**70.8 (1.6)**
Broughtons Waterhole on right (.1 km to actual waterhole) with some good camping. This waterhole is privately owned, however access is permitted by courtesy of the owners.

**70.9 (0.1)**
Major road junction — veer slightly to the right (heading east) on the continuation of the McDonald Highway. Broughtons Track and Mortat Track go off to left and right. Mt. Turner track is almost straight ahead veering slightly to left.
  It is a 2 km run to Mt. Turner and worth the diversion. It is no mountain, by any stretch of the imagination, but it is the highest thing around and offers good views of the surrounding desert.

**75.1 (4.2)**
Signpost on right 'Chinamans Flat'.

**77.7 (2.6)**
Cross Roads — PSA. LH & RH track is Central Avenue going north/south.

**82.0 (4.3)**
Track junction — PSA. LH track is Boar Track, RH track Fenceline Track.

**84.7 (2.7)**
Pass through a swamp area. There is a diversion track to the left going around it just before you hit the swamp area.

**86.6 (1.9)**
Track on right — PSA. RH track is Sand Track.

**87.3 (0.7)**
Track on right — PSA. RH track is Brooks Track which leads to Brooks Dam water point.

**90.0 (2.7)**
Track on left — turn left onto Stans Camp Track going north/south. McDonald Highway continues straight ahead.
  Stans Camp Track is possibly one of the oldest tracks in the Little Desert and was established about 1885.

**93.5 (3.5)**
Track on right — turn right onto Crater Track.

**94.7 (1.2)**
Track on left — PSA. LH track Whimpeys Track.

**96.8 (2.1)**
View of crater on right. There are a couple of small camping spots around this section of the track.
  There are some good views coming down from the crater area overlooking Mt. Araplies on the right and the Little Desert National Park in front.

**98.0 (1.2)**
T-junction — turn left onto the Old Nhill Road.

**98.1 (0.1)**
Y-Junction — veer right onto Red Gum Track. The LH fork is the continuation of the Old Nhill Road.

**102.0 (3.9)**
Beginning of the Red Gum Swamp area.

**103.0 (1.0)**
Main Red Gum swamp area.

**103.1 (0.1)**
Water on right and some very pleasant camping sites.

**103.4 (0.3)**
Faint track on left — PSA.

**104.3 (0.9)**
Faint track on left — PSA. LH track rejoins the main track about 1 km further on.

**105.5 (1.2)**
Faint cross roads — PSA.

**105.7 (0.2)**
Track veers to the left.

**105.9 (0.2)**
Track on left — turn left. Back on bitumen.

**108.3 (2.4)**
Track on right — turn right. Track follows a fence line on your left.

**109.8 (1.5)**
T-junction — turn right. RH track SP 'Jungkum Track'.

**110.0 (0.2)**
Y-junction — veer left continuing on Jungkum Track.

**115.2 (5.2)**
T-junction — turn left onto Link Track. RH is continuation of the Jungkum Track.

**119.0 (3.8)**
T-junction — turn right onto Dahlenburgs Mill Track.

**119.1 (0.1)**
Dahlenburgs Mill on right. Tank/windmill still in use. If you get out and have a look you'll see what's left of an extremely old trough — a reminder of the early days when they tried to graze sheep in the desert.

**120.3 (1.2)**
T-junction — veer right along the Dahlenburgs Mill Track. LH track is Mathews Track.

**123.7 (3.4)**
Y-Junction — veer left continuing on Dahlenburgs Mill Track. RH track is Salt Lake Track. View of Salt Lakes directly in front.

**124.1 (0.4)**
Track on right — veer right on Dahlenburgs Mill Track. Salt Lake Track continues straight ahead.

**126.3 (2.2)**
Track on left — PSA. LH track is Centre Track.
    This section of track would be very boggy when wet — use caution.

**127.4 (1.1)**
Track on right and camp area — PSA. RH track leads into the Bushwalkers Overnight Camping area. The camping area is 100 metres in from the track with a few small swamps and dams around making for an excellent camp setting.

**129.9 (2.5)**
Track on left — veer left continuing on Dahlenburgs Mill Track. RH track leads to a water point.
    Almost immediately after this track junction you hit a major track junction —
    Track junction — turn left onto the Mallee Track. RH track is the continuation of the Dahlenburgs Mill Track.

**135.4 (5.5)**
T-junction — turn right onto the McCabes Hut Track. LH track, just after you turn, leads to a water point.

**142.7 (7.3)**
Track on left — PSA — passing the Eagle Swamp on the left. LH track is Dry Well Track.

**143.5 (0.8)**
Track on left — PSA. LH track is Eagle Swamp Track which skirts around the top edge of the swamp. Approx. 0.2 kms up this track is some nice camping with lots of shade trees.

**143.6 (0.1)**
Track on right — PSA.

**144.6 (1.0)**
Track on right — PSA.

**144.8 (0.2)**
Track Junction — turn right. SP 'Dimboola'.

**144.9 (0.1)**
Faint track on left — PSA. LH track leads into swamp area.

**145.6 (0.7)**
Sign on right '4WDs Only'.

**145.7 (0.1)**
T-junction — turn left. SP on right 'McCabes Hut Track'.

**145.8 (0.1)**
Track junction — turn right through gate. SP left 'Little Desert National Park. (Dogs, cats, firearms are prohibited)'. LH track continues on to Dimboola.
    Once through gate turn hard left.

**146.2 (0.4)**
Track on left — turn left.

**146.3 (0.1)**
Ellis Crossing on the Wimmera River.
    There are a number of tracks going both left and right of the main track after Ellis Crossing. Down which you'll find some excellent camping spots along the Wimmera River.

**146.5 (0.2)**
Track on left — PSA.

**148.1 (1.6)**
Pass farmhouse — PSA on the West Wail Road.

**148.3 (0.2)**
Track on right — PSA. RH track leads down to West Wail State Forest.

**154.1 (5.8)**
Cross Roads — PSA. Back on bitumen.

**157.8 (3.7)**
T-junction — at the Great Western Highway. Turn right into Pimpinio township. (Track you have just come off is signposted at this T-junction 'West Wail').

# MT. TUGWELL THE HARD WAY

This short trek, just south of Warburton, has a little bit of everything. The first hill is a ripper and most will find it a great challenge. After that the challenges still keep coming, but they're different and not so intense.

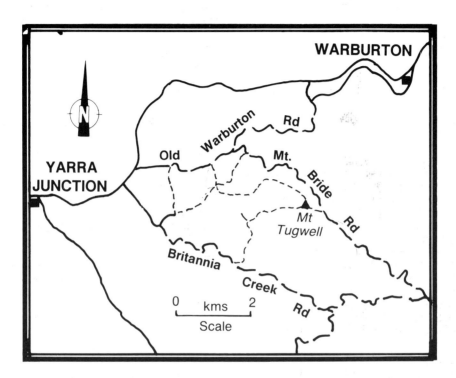

## STANDARD
Hard to very hard. This trek is only recommended for experienced drivers and those that have a well set up rig.

## DISTANCE and TIME
This trek starts at Wesburn, some 50 kms east of Melbourne and just five to six kilometres west of Warburton.

Trek distance is 15 kms and it can be done in one to one and a half hours — if you're lucky!

## RECOMMENDED MAPS/GUIDES
Vicmap's 1:25,000 Gladysdale covers the area of the trek, but some tracks, such as the first one straight up the hill, are not marked.

## RESTRICTIONS/PERMITS REQUIRED
A number of tracks are closed off in this area during winter, although generally the route described is open all year.

*ult. route moved to left* TR *Cemetery fire totally thro ... up till top w/...over! 4.5 km to end back on main TL TO go back*

# TREK

**0.0 (0.0)**
Road junction of Warburton Highway and Old Warburton Road — road on right — turn right onto the Old Warburton Road.

**1.0 (1.0)**
Bitumen ends, road turns to dirt. *closed*

**1.1 (0.1)**
Major road junction — various tracks both left and right. Proceed straight ahead (PSA) on minor dirt track heading straight up the hill. The Old Warburton Road veers round to the left. Track up hill is interesting and a fairly hard drive as the track is badly eroded, rutted and extremely steep, with very loose rocks making traction difficult. *closed went rt, then left up hill*

**1.6 (0.5)**
Track on left — PSA.

**1.8 (0.2)**
T-junction — turn left. You've reached the top of the hill and the worse is over!

**1.9 (0.1)**
Y-junction — veer right.

**2.5 (0.6)** *very rutted !!!*
Junction with logging coup (large cleared area) — continue straight ahead through the cleared area, past a large clump of trees in the middle of the coup. Numerous tracks in this area. *3 tracks ↓ turn back*

**2.7 (0.2)**
Hit track on far side of clearing — turn right.

**2.9 (0.2)**
Y-junction — veer left.

**3.1 (0.2)**
Track veers round to the left and continues up the hill. Straight in front, before veering left, is a large fenced area.
   The track up the hill is deeply rutting and eroded, but not all that steep. However in wet conditions it would be extremely slippery.

**4.9 (1.8)**
Y-junction — veer left.

**5.5 (0.6)**
Good views to the left looking down into the valley.

**5.7 (0.2)**
Track on right — PSA.

**6.3 (0.6)**
Track on right — turn right onto Justice Track. Lefthand (LH) track continues for 600 metres and hits the main Mount Bride Road.
   After cresting Mt. Tugwell, Justice Track becomes steep and is extremely slippery in wet conditions.

**7.4 (1.1)**
Track on left — veer right continuing on main track.

**8.6 (1.2)**
Track on right — veer left continuing on main track.

**9.2 (0.6)**
Track on left — veer right.

**9.8 (0.6)**
Faint track on left — PSA.

**10.0 (0.2)**
Faint track on left — main track veers hard right.

**10.2 (0.2)**
Faint track on right — PSA. Cross Britannia Creek soon afterwards.

**10.3 (0.1)**
T-junction with main Britannia Creek Road — turn right.

**10.6 (0.3)**
Track on left (fairly overgrown) — PSA.

**11.5 (0.9)**
Track on left — PSA.

**12.7 (1.2)**
Quarry on left — PSA.

**12.9 (0.2)**
Y-junction — veer right. LH track SP 'Buffer Break Track'.

**13.3 (0.4)**
Y-junction — veer right keeping on Britannia Creek Road which now becomes bitumen.

**13.7 (0.4)**
T-junction — turn left following main road.

**15.0 (1.3)**
T-junction with Warburton Highway — turn left for Melbourne.

# YARRA GLEN TO MURRINDINDI SCENIC RESERVE

The forests north of Yarra Glen are rich in variety with a profusion of plants, birds and animals.

Mountain ash, cherished and logged for its fine light timber, is grow at the higher elevations, while messmate, mountain grey gum and manna gum are the predominant species on the lower foothills and slopes of this region of the Great Dividing Range. Much of this forest area is regrowth after the devastating forest fires of 1939. Other sections have been logged in the recent past and it is interesting to note the regeneration that has occurred in the last 10–20 years.

Many of the trees in this area of Victoria reach outstanding heights. While early pioneers recorded giants up to 120 metres tall, a number of 55 year old trees are already over 75 metres in height when measured just a few years ago.

Logging is still carried out in these rich forests, so log trucks and heavy machinery are often encountered on the roads and tracks. Take care!

The Murrindindi area is not only an excellent camping spot, there are a number of historic sites worth a visit. The Dindi Mill Site, passed on this trek, is one, and it's worth a short stop and time to explore.

The Murrindindi Scenic Reserve, with its many well setup and maintained camping areas, its excellent walks and its reasonable trout fishing, is an ideal place to camp for a day or two.

The Murrindindi River Walk extends for a distance of 11.3 kms along the length of the Reserve, from the suspension bridge in the north to the Murrindindi Cascades in the south. It links with a track leading from the Wilhelmina car park to the base of the Wilhelmina Falls, a distance of 1.8 kms. The track south of the Bull Creek area follows the route of an historic timber extraction tram way which operated prior to the devastating 1939 wild fire. Features include an intact section of tram line, a reconstructed bogey and an old saw mill site.

## STANDARD
Easy to moderate. Some of the tracks are a little overgrown, so take care.

## DISTANCE and TIME
Yarra Glen is 50 kms north-east of Melbourne and has all facilities for the traveller.

The trek is nearly 90 kms in length and ends some 35 kms north of Yarra Glen. It takes about three hours to drive the course, but it's better to take your time and enjoy the forest.

## RECOMMENDED MAPS/GUIDES
The Conservation Forests & Lands 1:100,000 Toolangi-Black Range is probably the best map, although some tracks and areas such as the Dindi Mill Site are not marked.

## CAMPING
A number of pleasant, established camping areas are located in the Murrindindi Scenic Reserve. A number of other places, in the forest, near streams, would also be suitable for a camp. Don't forget to obey all regulations regarding camping and fires.

## RESTRICTIONS/PERMITS REQUIRED
While a number of tracks in this area are closed over the winter months, the route detailed generally remains open.

## CAUTION
Log trucks use many of these roads during the working week and on weekends the area is popular with four wheelers and trail bike riders. Take care!

# TREK

**0.0 (0.0)**
Yarra Glen, 50 kms from Melbourne, in middle of town, heading north.

**16.3 (16.3)**
Cross roads — PSA. Toolangi and Healesville to right, King Lake to left.

**21.4 (5.1)**
Yea River Park sign on left.

**22.8 (1.4)**
Track on right — PSA.

**22.9 (0.1)**
Road on right — turn right, signposted (SP) 'Marginal Road'.

**23.0 (0.1)**
Track on left and large car park area — PSA. Lefthand (LH) track SP 'Glenburn Track'.

**25.7 (2.7)**
Track on left — PSA.

**26.0 (0.3)**
Cross roads — PSA. RH track is SP 'Wee Creek Track' and is the route of the tough "Rocky Track and The Steps" trek notes.

**28.2 (2.2)**
Track on left — PSA.

**28.4 (0.2)**
Track on left — PSA.

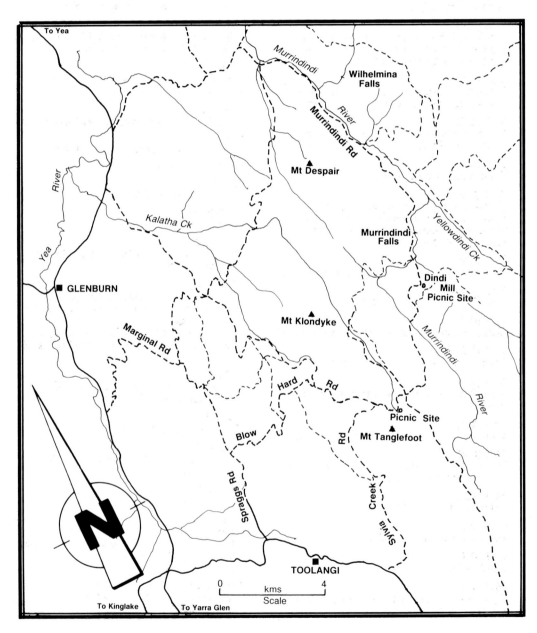

**28.6 (0.2)**
Track on left — PSA.

**29.4 (0.8)**
Y-junction — veer right, SP 'Marginal Road'. LH fork SP 'Eagle Nest Road'.

**31.4 (2.0)**
Major track junction — PSA, veering slightly to the left, on Spraggs Road (SP). Marginal Road veers round sharply to the left. First RH track is SP 'Victoria Range Road', then you have another faint (overgrown) track on your right.

**31.9 (0.5)**
Track on left — PSA. LH track SP 'Gutter Creek Track'. The track along this section follows a creek with some very nice tree ferns and gum trees.

**32.8 (0.9)**
Track on left — PSA. Immediately after track on left you have a T-junction — turn right, SP 'Criss Cross Road'.

**32.9 (0.1)**
Track on your left — turn left. This track is narrow at times and fairly overgrown.

**34.1 (1.2)**
Cross roads — turn left onto main dirt track — Downie Road.

**35.0 (0.9)**
Faint cross tracks — PSA.

**37.2 (2.2)**
Cross roads — turn right, SP 'Downies Spur Track'. This track can be quite boggy in wet conditions, but passes through some very nice timber.

**39.1 (1.9)**
Y-junction — turn left, SP 'Sams Hut Track'.

**39.2 (0.1)**
Faint track on right — PSA.

**39.9 (0.7)**
Cross roads — turn left, SP 'Nolans Road'.

**40.9 (1.0)**
Faint track on left — PSA on main track.

**41.5 (0.6)**
T-junction — turn right, SP 'Blowhard Road'.

**43.4 (1.9)**
Y-junction — veer left, SP 'Yea Link Road'.

**44.0 (0.6)**
Track on left — PSA on main road which veers round to the right.

**44.5 (0.5)**
Track on left — PSA.

**45.0 (0.5)**
Faint track on left — PSA.

**45.1 (0.1)**
Track on right — PSA.

**46.7 (1.6)**
T-junction — turn left, SP 'Sylvia Creek Road' — a major dirt road.

**46.9 (0.2)**
Track on right — PSA. Sign on left 'Regrowth Area From the 1939 Fires'. There are numerous tracks along this section — continue on the main road.

**50.2 (3.3)**
Track on right — PSA. RH track SP 'Myrtle Creek Road'.

**50.4 (0.2)**
Track on left — PSA. LH track SP 'Blowhard Road'. Now travelling through an area of Mountain Ash, established in 1972, regenerated after logging.

**51.4 (1.0)**
Track on right is the Mt. Tanglefoot/Mt. St. Leonard Walking Circuit. Also a large car parking/picnic area on right — PSA.

**52.4 (1.0)**
Major road junction — turn left, SP 'Kalatha Road'. RH track SP 'Hardy Road'.

**53.6 (1.2)**
Y-junction — veer right onto the Top Kalatha Road.

**55.8 (2.2)**
T-junction — turn right, SP 'Kalatha Road'.

**56.6 (0.8)**
Track on right — PSA. RH track SP 'Woodmore Road'.

**56.7 (0.1)**
Track on right — PSA.

**56.8 (0.1)**
Track on left — PSA.

**57.6 (0.8)**
Y-junction — veer right. LH fork SP 'Mt. Despair Road'.

**59.4 (1.8)**
Y-junction — veer left, joining Dindi River Road which comes in on your right just after the Y-junction.
   If you veer right and continue for 200 meters you'll find a small cleared camping area on the creek.

**60.3 (0.9)**
T-junction — turn right. LH track SP 'Horseyard Creek Road'.

**60.4 (0.1)**
Faint track on left — PSA.

**60.8 (0.4)**
Track on right — PSA on main track, veering left.

**60.9 (0.1)**
Track on left — PSA.

**61.8 (0.9)**
Major T-junction — turn right onto Murrindindi Road (SP) and cross Murrindindi River — Egans Bridge.

**64.1 (2.3)**
Track on left — turn left, SP 'Winch Road' and 'Dindi Mill Site 500 metres'.

**64.4 (0.3)**
Track on left — PSA.

**64.5 (0.1)**
Picnic Area and site of old Dindi Mill —
PSA. The picnic area has tables, BBQs and
toilet facilities for day use only — no
camping.

**64.8 (0.3)**
Y-junction — veer right.

**65.6 (0.8)**
Cross Yellowdindi Creek — old logged
bridge.

**65.7 (0.1)**
Y-junction — veer right, SP 'Bull Creek
Road'.

**66.0 (0.3)**
Y-junction — veer left, continuing on Bull
Creek Road. RH fork is SP 'Spur Link
Road'.

**66.4 (0.4)**
Track on left — PSA on Bull Creek Road.
LH track is SP 'Rocky Mouth Road'.

**66.6 (0.2)**
Y-junction — veer left, continuing on main
track.

**68.0 (1.4)**
Track on left — turn left.

**68.4 (0.4)**
Creek crossing — beware of the old logged
bridge, watch for holes.

**68.6 (0.2)**
T-junction — turn left, continuing on Bull
Creek Road. RH track is SP 'Spur Road'.

**69.3 (0.7)**
Track on left — PSA.

**69.6 (0.3)**
Track on left — PSA and immediately cross
the creek — logged bridge, but watch for
the holes.

**69.7 (0.1)**
Track on right — PSA, continuing on main
track which veers round to the left.

**69.8 (0.1)**
Track on right — PSA.

**70.2 (0.4)**
Faint track on left — PSA.

**70.9 (0.7)**
Track on right — PSA.

**71.0 (0.1)**
Track on left — PSA.

**71.1 (0.1)**
Track on right — PSA.

**71.2 (0.1)**
Track on right — PSA. RH track marked S
Creek Road.

**71.3 (0.1)**
Track on left — PSA. LH track SP 'Winch
Road — road is closed, walkers only'.

**72.6 (1.3)**
Track on right — PSA.

**73.6 (1.0)**
Cross Murrindindi River — bridged. After
crossing you have the Bull Creek Camping
Area on the right and the Murrindindi River
Walking track.

**73.9 (0.3)**
T-junction — turn right onto Murrindindi
Road.

**74.5 (0.6)**
Track on right — PSA. RH track leads to
the Ferns Camping Area.

**74.7 (0.2)**
Track on right — PSA. RH track SP 'Falls
Creek Road' and also leads to camping
area.
   There are numerous roads, on the right,
along this section of the Murrindindi Scenic
Reserve. Many of the roads lead to camping
areas beside the Murrindindi River — 2WD
access.

**75.8 (1.1)**
Track on right — PSA. RH track leads to
Water Gate Camping Area.

**76.9 (1.1)**
Viewing area on right out to Wilhelmina
Falls.

**77.6 (0.7)**
Wilhelmina Falls day parking area on right
and walking track to falls — PSA.

**78.3 (0.7)**
Track on right and picnic area — PSA.

**78.6 (0.3)**
Track on right — PSA. RH track leads to
Pinetree Camping area.

**79.0 (0.4)**
Track on right — PSA. RH track leads to
camping area.

**79.4 (0.4)**
Track on right — PSA. RH track is the
Jackson Mill track, which crosses the
Murrindindi River — not bridged.

**80.1 (0.7)**
Road on left — PSA past the saw mill on
your left, continuing on main road.

**82.8 (2.7)**
Y-junction — veer left, SP to 'Glenburn'.

**88.0 (5.2)**
T-junction with the Yarra Glen Yea Road —
turn left to Melbourne 85 km.

# THE NORTHERN OTWAYS

Much of the first section of this trek is through the Alcoa lease area, inland from the seaside resort of Anglesea. Alcoa, the multi-national aluminium smelter giant, operates a coal pit and a power station here as an emergency power supply for its Portland plant.

Once away from the rural plains south of Geelong, the forest consists of smallish gums such as stringybark and peppermint. For the first few kilometres the track borders a swamp and heath area that in spring can be rich in flowers.

Further south, the forests are wetter and the trees larger, with a much denser undergrowth. Along the top of most of the ridges messmate, blue gum and grey gum predominate, with myrtle beech and blackwood being found in the moist gullies.

Birdlife is common and varied. Animal life too is rich and for those taking their time along these tracks black wallabies will often be seen.

## STANDARD
Very dependent on the weather. If it's been dry for some time the trek is easy. If it's been raining, expect a lot of fun and mud. You really should travel in company with somebody else and have a good range of recovery gear.

## DISTANCE and TIME
Trek starts 15 kms south of Geelong, about one to one and a half hours south of Melbourne. Less than 100 kms later will see you at Aireys Inlet on the coast. If it's dry it will take one and a half to two hours. If it's wet, you may decide not to go all the way!!

## RECOMMENDED MAPS/GUIDES
The Conservation Forests & Lands 1:125,000 Otways Forest Map is probably the best single map of the area, although track detail within the Alcoa lease area is poor.

## RESTRICTIONS/PERMITS REQUIRED
While tracks do get closed off in the Otways during winter, this route remains officially open all year.

## CAUTION
This area is popular with trail bike riders — take care!

## TREK
Trek begins 15 kms south of Geelong, on the Princess Highway.

**0.0 (0.0)**
Cross roads — Princess Highway and the Cape Otway Road — turn left, heading to Cape Otway. Signposted (SP) 'Moriac 6/Cape Otway Road'.

**5.2 (5.2)**
Railway crossing (centre of Moriac). Cross railway line and turn left, SP 'Torquay 23/Anglesea 30'.

**8.8 (3.6)**
Road on right — turn right, SP 'Larcombes Road/Gravel Pit'.

**9.7 (0.9)**
Road on left — turn left, SP 'Forest Road/Gravel Pit'.

**18.3 (8.6)**
Road on right — turn right, SP 'Gum Flats Road'.

**19.5 (1.2)**
Track on left — turn left, SP 'Harrison Track'.

**19.6 (0.1)**
Track on left — PSA. The track now borders a large swamp area on the right.

**21.8 (2.2)**
Creek crossing (usually with some water in it).

**22.7 (0.9)**
Small creek crossing.

**23.0 (0.3)**
Extremely boggy section to negotiate — especially in wet conditions.

**23.1 (0.1)**
End of boggy section.

**24.0 (0.9)**
Creek crossing — can be quite boggy.

**25.3 (1.3)**
Track on left — continue on main track which veers round sharply to the right on top of the hill.

**25.4 (0.1)**
Long, boggy section — can be difficult in
wet conditions.

**25.5 (0.1)**
Track on left — continue on main track
which veers round sharply to the right.

**25.6 (0.1)**
Track on left — PSA.

**26.9 (1.3)**
Track on left — continue on main track
which veers round to the right.

**27.6 (0.7)**
T-junction — turn right and cross causeway
at the bottom end of a swamp.

**27.7 (0.1)**
T-junction — turn left. Next 100 metres is
steep and eroded.

**27.8 (0.1)**
Track on right — continue on main track
which veers left, following fenceline on your
left.

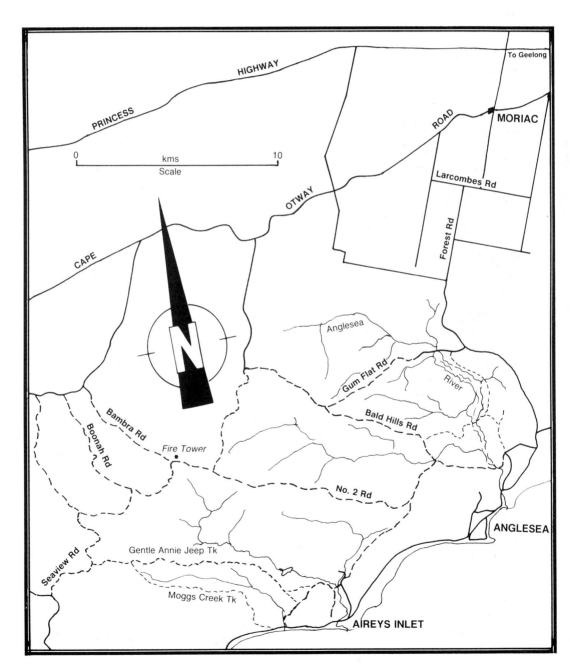

**28.3 (0.5)**
Track on left — turn left, up a steep little pinch and then be prepared to immediately turn right or you'll go through a fence and into a large dam. At the top of the hill you've got good views overlooking the Alcoa Coal Mine.

Follow the track around to your right at the top of the hill, following the fenceline on your left.

**28.6 (0.3)**
Track on right — PSA.

**28.7 (0.1)**
Track on left — PSA.

**29.1 (0.4)**
Track on left — PSA. The next section of track is across deep, soft sand.

**29.4 (0.3)**
Track on right — PSA. Reached the top of the hill and end of sandy section.

**30.1 (0.7)**
Faint track on left — PSA.

**30.4 (0.3)**
Faint track on right — PSA.

**30.7 (0.3)**
Track on right — PSA.

**31.4 (0.7)**
Good views on the top of the ridge to the left overlooking the Alcoa Lease mining area and the township of Anglesea and the ocean.

**31.6 (0.2)**
Major T-junction — turn left onto main dirt road.

**32.9 (1.3)**
Track on right — PSA. Righthand (RH) track SP 'Salt Creek Track'.

There are numerous tracks along this section — continue on main dirt road.

**33.9 (1.0)**
Dirt road on left — PSA.

**35.0 (1.1)**
Y-junction — veer right, SP 'No. 2 Road'.

Turning left at either of the last two road junctions will take you back into Anglesea.

**35.2 (0.2)**
Y-junction — veer right.

**36.3 (1.1)**
Track on right — PSA. RH track SP 'Denham Track'.

**39.0 (2.7)**
Angahook State Park sign on left.

**39.1 (0.1)**
Track on left — continue on main track which veers round slightly to the right. Lefthand (LH) track SP 'Batson Track'.

**42.9 (3.8)**
Cross roads — PSA. LH road SP 'Bambra Road', RH road SP 'Breakfast Creek Road'.

**45.7 (2.8)**
Track on right — PSA. RH track SP 'Hammonds Road' and 'Angahook Lorne State Park' sign on right.

**47.3 (1.6)**
Fire Tower on right — PSA.

**47.7 (0.4)**
Track on left — turn left, SP 'Boonah Road'.

**50.9 (3.2)**
Dirt road on left — turn left.

**54.3 (3.4)**
Track on left — turn left, SP 'Seaview Road — Dry Weather Road Only'.

**57.8 (3.5)**
Track on left — turn left, SP 'Gentle Annie Track/Moggs Creek Track'.

**59.9 (2.1)**
Track on right — PSA. RH track SP 'Moggs Creek Track'.

**64.1 (4.2)**
Track on left — PSA. LH track SP 'Ironbark Spur Track'.

**67.9 (3.8)**
Walking track (SP) on left and right — PSA.

**68.4 (0.5)**
Y-junction — veer left, continue following fenceline on your left.

**69.4 (1.0)**
T-junction — turn left, SP 'Old Coach Road'.

Numerous tracks off the Old Coach Road — PSA along road towards Aireys Inlet.

**71.2 (1.8)**
Y-junction — veer left and cross bridge.

**71.7 (0.5)**
T-junction — turn right — hit bitumen. Continue on the main road towards Aireys Inlet.

**73.6 (1.9)**
T-junction with the Great Ocean Road — turn right for Aireys Inlet, left for Anglesea and Geelong.

# THE OMEO COACH ROAD

Once it linked the coastal part of Port Albert to the gold fields around Omeo. Cobb and Co. coaches rattled across a road that in the end was a better track than it is today.

In 1852, when the Omeo fields were just beginning, the cost of getting goods to Omeo from Port Albert was around 50 pounds per tonne — a very large sum of money. As the fields took on a semblance of permanence and other fields in the region were discovered, access was improved. While this trek takes in only a short section of the original road, the workmanship and effort that went into it can be plainly seen.

Along the way you'll pass close to the ruins of other gold mines and towns born to the tune of gold.

This is a magnificent part of Victoria's high country. Mountain streams, dense forest and beautiful sweeping views are all part and parcel of this trip.

## STANDARD
Fairly easy throughout the length of the trip, with the river crossings generally very shallow.

## DISTANCE and TIME
Swifts Creek, the start point, is some 95 km north of the Gippsland town of Bairnsdale. Bairnsdale itself is 281 kms (3 hrs driving) west of Melbourne. The trek is just over 60 km long and takes approximately 4 hours. The trek finishes just 60 km north of Bairnsdale.

While you can do the trek in about 4 hours of easy driving, it should be part of a weekend or longer jaunt through this magnificent area. If you're into fossicking around old mine sites you could spend days.

## RECOMMENDED MAPS/GUIDES
The 1:100,000 Map Omeo covers this trek.

## CAMPING
There are a number of spots ideal for camping along this route. Stop and enjoy them and please leave them clean of rubbish.

## RESTRICTIONS/PERMITS REQUIRED
For some of the time this trek passes through private property. Leave gates as you find them; do not leave the road and be aware of wandering stock.

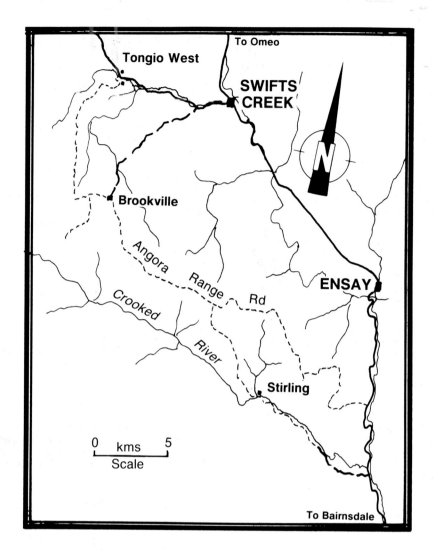

## TREK

### 0.0 (0.0)
Swifts Creek Post Office — cross roads. Take road heading west, past the milkbar and supermarket.

### 9.7 (9.7)
Track on left — turn left. Lefthand (LH) track is Charlotte Spur Track.

### 10.1 (0.4)
Creek crossing.

### 10.2 (0.1)
Track on left — PSA. LH track leads into old mine.

### 10.3 (0.1)
Just after hill, on the left a little way up the hill, there is an old ruin of the Battery House on the Water Race. You will need to get out and walk a short distance.

### 11.2 (0.9)
Reed area on your right which is where the gold dredge finished.

### 11.5 (0.3)
Y-Junction — veer left, along the original stage road. Righthand (RH) track goes up to the old mining area and mullock heaps of the Cassilis Mine.

### 12.0 (0.5)
Pass through fence line and gate. Signposted (SP) 'Private Property', but the road is actually a gazetted road. Do not leave track.

### 12.7 (0.7)
Track veers to the left. Directly in front is a gate and house. Track follows fenceline alongside house on your right. Track is very faint.

### 12.8 (0.1)
Track veers to the right, along cutting on left. There is a small water tank on your right at this point.

### 13.4 (0.6)
Along this section is a very good example of the old stone supporting wall for the road. It is well worth stopping to have a look.

60

**15.3 (1.9)**
Faint trail on your left — PSA. LH trail was a miner's trail that goes down into Rileys Creek — walking track only, and it is private property.

**15.4 (0.1)**
Pass through fence line and gate.

**15.7 (0.3)**
Area on your left is the top end of the Lady McGregor Mine. Beware there are some dangerous shafts is this area. The cleared area on the left was known as Gum Forest and was worked mainly by Scottish people. There was also a water wheel on this site — the first in the area.

**16.5 (0.8)**
Two big fence posts on right — track on your left (private road) — PSA. A walking track on the right leads down to the Upper Swifts Creek mining area. Some good ruins, waterwheel site, some buildings — approx. 1 hr walk one way.

**17.9 (1.4)**
Pass through fence line and gate. Remember that you are still passing through private property. Beware of stock on road.

**18.5 (0.6)**
Small creek crossing — bridged.

**18.7 (0.2)**
Pass through fence line and gate. Dam on both left and right.

**19.2 (0.5)**
Pass through fence line and gate.

**19.5 (0.3)**
Pass old homestead on right and left.

**22.3 (2.8)**
T-junction — turn right, joining the Brookvale Road.

**22.6 (0.3)**
Track on left (Dorothy Cutting Road) — turn left into Angoora Forest Drive, SP 'Rough Road Conditions. Beware Log Trucks'.
   Along the beginning of this track was the site of the old mining town of Brookvale.

**22.9 (0.3)**
SP 'Dorothy Cutting'.

**25.3 (2.4)**
Track on right — PSA. RH track SP 'Ezard Track' which leads down the Highland Chief Mine — about 3 kms in. Beware of dangerous shafts in this area. There is a delightful tree fern forest about half way in.

**26.5 (1.2)**
Track on left — turn left, continuing on the Angoora Range Road. Straight ahead will take you to Dargo.

**27.7 (1.2)**
Water point on left.

**27.9 (0.2)**
Track on left — PSA. LH track SP 'Christmas Bridge Gordon's Track'.

**28.8 (0.9)**
Track on left — PSA. LH track SP 'Sargent's Track'.

**30.4 (1.6)**
Track on left — PSA. LH track SP 'D7 Track'.

**31.3 (0.9)**
Cross roads — PSA. RH track SP 'Clarke's Track'. LH track SP 'Burwood Road'.

**32.6 (1.3)**
Track on right — PSA. RH track SP 'Dawson City Track and Track closed at Haunted Stream — June 15 to October 31'.

**32.8 (0.2)**
Track on left — PSA. LH track is Aub's Road.

**33.7 (0.9)**
Track on right — turn right.

**34.8 (1.1)**
Track on right — PSA. RH track is Dugout Track.

**40.3 (5.5)**
Track on left — PSA. LH track leads to Regnans Gully Fireplace and Dam. Also a couple of faint logging tracks along this section.

**41.3 (1.0)**
Track on right  — turn right onto Stirling Track.
   Track on right just after turning — PSA, continuing on the Stirling Track. RH track is the Sunshine Mottle Track which is closed at the Haunted Stream Track from June 15 — October 31.

**42.2 (0.9)**
Y-Junction — veer right.

**45.8 (3.6)**
Track drops steeply here and again just before the next track junction.

**49.6 (3.8)**
Track junction — PSA. Haunted Stream Track comes in sharply off to the right. This track has approximately 45 river crossings and is suitable only for experienced driver.
   The Victoria Mine track also comes in sharply on the left and it is well worth a short detour to explore the Victoria Mine area. There are still quite a few ruins of old huts and chimneys along the track in. About 700 metres in from the junction you'll pass the actual Victoria Mine Tunnel. There are some old gold carts and mining pieces still lying around the area which are worth looking at.
   Just after the Haunted Stream and Victoria Mine track junctions the main track veers sharply to the right across a bridge. There is a small, but very nice camping area on your left, just before the bridge crossing.

**49.8 (0.2)**
Track on right — PSA. RH track leads back onto Engineer's Spur.

Along this section there are the remains of the old pub (a rock wall) and the coach house area. There is also some reasonable camping here.

**49.9 (0.1)**
Track on right — PSA, continuing on the Haunted Stream Road which veering left. RH track is Five Mile Spur Road.

**51.1 (1.2)**
Creek crossing — bridged.

**51.7 (0.6)**
Cleared area on right. New mining operation. Used to be called 'Baylis Flat'.

**52.3 (0.6)**
Track on left — PSA. Possible camping spot. Beware — there are a lot private roads along this section leading to mining areas.

**54.4 (2.1)**
Creek crossing — bridged.

**60.1 (5.7)**
Track on right — PSA. RH track is Conn's Track.

**61.4 (1.3)**
Pass through fence line and gate.

**62.6 (1.2)**
Pass through fence line and gate. SP 'Public Gate'. Beware of Stock. Stockyards on right. Just after passing through the gate you pass a house on your right.

**62.8 (0.2)**
T-junction — turn left onto the bitumen for Swifts Creek (36 kms north) or turn right to Bairnsdale (58 kms south).

# ELDORADO GOLD TO PICTURESQUE YACK

This is one of our favorite areas in Victoria and we have spent many a pleasant day enjoying the cool waters of Reedy Creek and the hills and valleys between historic Beechworth and Yackandandah.

There is some fine camping along Reedy Creek and the normally shallow waters of this stream makes a top spot to cool off on a summers day. For those a little more energetic the river is a playground for gold and gem enthusiasts and a few hours panning will always result in a flash of colour.

Once up around Beechworth the country and the vegetation changes and the run from here to Yackandandah along Nine MileCreek and Yackandandah Creek presents a different vista to that between Eldorado and Beechworth. The challenges are also different.

The area was once a mecca for gold seekers and many relics of the past can be found along the way. Near Eldorado the huge gold dredge is worth a look, as are the museums in both Eldorado and Beechworth. Through the forest there are many mine shafts and these, especially those behind Beechworth, can be bloody deep. Mullock heaps and the remains of where they sluiced and dredged for gold line most of the creeks in the area.

The forest east of Beechworth is much drier than the forests that stretch between Beechworth and Yackandandah where in the moist gullies treeferns can be found. With such a variety of vegetation there is a wealth of animals and birds.

For nature lovers spring and early summer are the best times while any time is good to find gold.

## STANDARD
This trek is of a moderate standard. When the tracks behind Beechworth are wet they can be a bit slippery! Between Eldorado and Beechworth the trek is of an easy standard.

## DISTANCE AND TIME
Wangaratta is 250kms north of Melbourne along the Hume Highway, taking just 3 hours travelling.

The trek as detailed is 70kms long and takes 3 - 4 hours. However it is best to take at least a day and even longer. You can camp along the way or even stop in Beechworth as this trek passes right through the heart of this magic mountain town.

## RECOMMENDED MAPS/GUIDES
The best map is the Beechworth and District map produced by S.R. Brookes and available from good map shops. The Auslig 1:100,000 map 'Albury' covers the entire route of the trek.

## CAMPING
There is plenty of spots to camp along Reedy Creek and Nine Mile Creek.

## RESTRICTIONS
The tracks behind Beechworth are occasionally subject to closure. Check with the CNR office in Wangaratta, Ph: (057)28 1501.

## TREK

**0.0 (0.0)**
Road Junction. 4kms north of Wangaratta, SP Bright - Turn right (TR).

**0.5 (0.5)**
Road junction, SP Eldorado - Turn left (TL).

**2.5 (2.0)**
Road junction - veer right towards Eldorado

**15.3 (12.8)**
Road on left, signposted (SP) Byawatha/dredge - TL. By proceeding straight ahead (PSA) at this junction you would soon enter the township of Eldorado.

**15.6 (0.3)**
Bridge with parking area on right. From here it is an easy walk to the monster gold dredge that once worked this creek - it's worth a look.

**15.8 (0.2)**
Road Junction - turn half right.

**16.2 (0.4)**
Road junction - TR onto Old Coach Road.

**17.0 (0.8)**
Enter Mt Pilot Forest Park.

**19.4 (2.4)**
Track on left leads a short distance to pleasant campsite. PSA

**21.4 (2.0)**
Track on right - TR. Ramsey Track.

**23.9 (2.5)**
T-junction - TL and continue along this main track.

**24.9 (1.0)**
Track junction - Cross roads. Turn hard right.

**25.6 (0.7)**
Track on right leads to campsite. PSA

**27.4 (1.8)**
Creek crossing. There is a lot of old diggings and some ruins around this spot, once known as Napoleon Flat. You'll even find a good campsite and the area is popular with fossickers.

**27.7 (0.3)**
Track on left - PSA.

**28.7 (1.0)**
Faint track on right leads down to Reedy Creek. - PSA.

**29.9 (1.2)**
T-junction -TL onto main dirt road, 'Woolshed Road'. Right leads down to main crossing of Reedy Creek and back to the small township of Eldorado, approx 8kms.

For the next few kilometres there are a number of tracks off to the right leading down to the creek and to some excellent campsites.

**31.2 (1.3)**
Picnic area on right.

**32.9 (1.7)**
Reedy Creek Rd. on left - PSA.

**33.6 (0.7)**
Gladstone Tk. on left - PSA.

**36.8 (3.2)**
Warners Tk. on left - PSA.

**38.2 (1.4)**
Track junction - PSA to Woolshed. Left leads to Beechworth.

**38.4 (0.2)**
Reedy Creek crossing. This is a sandy but generally very easy crossing. Some good camp sites close to crossing on both sides of creek. From just past this point camping spots are a little thin on the ground.

**38.5 (0.1)**
T-junction - TL.

**39.8 (1.3)**
Track on left - PSA. Left hand track leads down to creek and past the remains of the Reedy Creek Powerhouse.

**42.3 (2.5)**
Track on right - PSA.

**42.5 (0.2)**
Road junction. Left leads to Woolshed Falls and the well set-up picnic area. It is worth some time to explore this spot. PSA towards Beechworth.

**44.0 (1.5)**
T-junction - TR to Beechworth.

**46.2 (2.2)**
Road junction - VR.

**47.2 (1.0)**
Enter Beechworth. PSA on main road to centre of town.

**49.2 (2.0)**
Centre of town and cross roads. - TL. SP 'Forest Drive - to Myrtleford/Stanley'.

**Zero trip meter.**

**0.0 (0.0)**
Cross roads heading towards Stanley.

**0.7 (0.7)**
Road junction - TL to Stanley.

**5.8 (5.1)**
Road junction - TL. SP Hurdle Flat Rd./Lake Kerferd.

**6.6 (0.8)**
Track on right - PSA. Road turns to gravel soon after junction.

**7.5 (0.9)**
T-junction - take dog leg to left then right.

**8.2 (0.7)**
Large cleared camping area on left, SP Hurdle Flat Picnic Area - PSA.

**8.3 (0.1)**
Crossroads with Rawes Rd. - TL.

**9.7 (1.4)**
Track junction - TR. Track signposted 'Lower Nine Mile Rd./To Wallaby Mine'.

**10.2 (0.5)**
Y-junction - veer left. RH track leads a short distance to parking area above the remains of the Wallaby Mine, one of the largest gold producers in the area.

**11.2 (1.0)**
Y-junction - veer right.

**12.4 (1.2)**
Cross creek. This is Nine Mile Creek.

**13.3 (0.9)**
Track on right, SP 'Reserve Spur Tk.' - PSA.

**14.5 (1.2)**
T-junction, SP 'Jenkins Tk.' - TR.

**14.6 (0.3)**
Faint track on right leads to cleared grassy area good for a camp. No water. PSA.

**14.7 (0.1)**
Track on left - PSA. LH track lead down 600 metres to a cleared grassy area beside creek.

**15.0 (0.3)**
T-junction - TL onto Yack Gate Rd.

**15.8 (0.8)**
Track on left , creek crossing, followed immediately by a T-junction, SP 'Yack No 1 Link Rd.'. Turn left at T-junction. Track before creek leads to pleasant spot beside stream.

**16.4 (0.6)**
Grassy area on left beside creek - good for a camp. PSA.

**16.9 (0.5)**
Creek crossing. There is a track just before the crossing that leads off to some other camping spots.

**17.1 (0.2)**
Track on right - PSA. RH track leads to large cleared area beside creek.

**17.4 (0.3)**
Crossroads - PSA. Fenced water tank on left.

**18.4 (1.0)**
Track on right - PSA.

**19.6 (1.2)**
Parking area on right. Short walk to a historic gold mining gorge. PSA.

**20.1 (0.5)**
Y-junction - veer right onto bitumen.

**21.1 (1.0)**
Crossroads. TR to the centre of town.

**21.5 (0.4)**
The heart of Yackandandah.

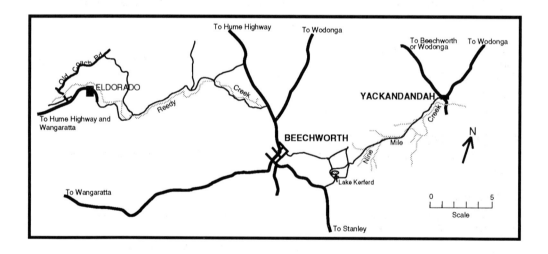

# PINK LAKES AND BEYOND

This trek begins and ends in the small hamlet of Murrayville, about 500 kms north-west of Melbourne and 300 kms east of Adelaide on the Ouyen Highway. This is the heart of Victoria's Mallee country. To the immediate north and south of the highway are the rolling wheat fields and farmlands of this rural region of Australia. Beyond these are the mallee wilderness areas of the Big Desert (to the south) and Sunset Country (to the north).

It is to Sunset Country that this trek takes you into. For much of it, the route passes through the Pink Lakes State Park. The most striking feature of this park is a group of salt pans which turn pink under certain conditions, but it is the vastness and solitude of the desert country which attracts us.

The park is exceptionally rich in plant life, including mallee, native pine, buloke, along with salt bush and porcupine grass.

While large animal life is not common, Red Kangaroos can sometimes be seen, making the region one of the few in Victoria where Red 'Roos roam.

Reptiles, especially lizards, are common, along with about 80 species of birds.

The area around Pink Lakes was taken up as a pastoral run in the late 1850's, but was abandoned by the 1890's. Salt harvesting began in 1916 and continued until 1975. The park was declared in 1979 and grazing phased out. Outside the park limited grazing still occurs on the public land.

Within the park there are a number of walking trails and a number of places worthy of a visit. Mount Crozier in the northern section of the park is worth climbing and this trek takes you right past it.

## STANDARD
Easy. There is some soft sand work and a few clay pans that only cause problems if they're wet.

## DISTANCE and TIME
Murrayville is about 500 kms north-west (and around 6 hours driving) from Melbourne and 300 kms east (3 1/2 — 4 hours driving) from Adelaide on the Ouyen Highway.

The trek as described is 183 kms and could be done in one day, but you wouldn't have time to enjoy the place. Slow down and stop a while!

## RECOMMENDED MAPS/GUIDES
The two AUSLIG 1:250,000 topographic maps Mildura and Ouyen are more than adequate for this trip.

## CAMPING
A pleasant camping are is located on the southern shores of Lake Crosbie. Limited water, toilets and fireplaces are provided.

There are plenty of other bush camping areas both in and outside the park.

No other facilities are available. Stores and fuel are obtainable at Murrayville or Underbool.

## RESTRICTIONS/PERMITS REQUIRED
Please stick to designated 4WD tracks and roads and do not go past any barriers.

Further information can be obtained from the National Parks and Wildlife Service Ranger based at Underbool, ph: (050) 94 6267.

## TREK

**0.0 (0.0)**
Murrayville Hotel — Ouyen Highway — heading east towards Ouyen.

**19.0 (19.0)**
Small settlement of Cowangie. Proceed straight ahead (PSA).

**39.4 (20.4)**
Cross railway line — PSA.

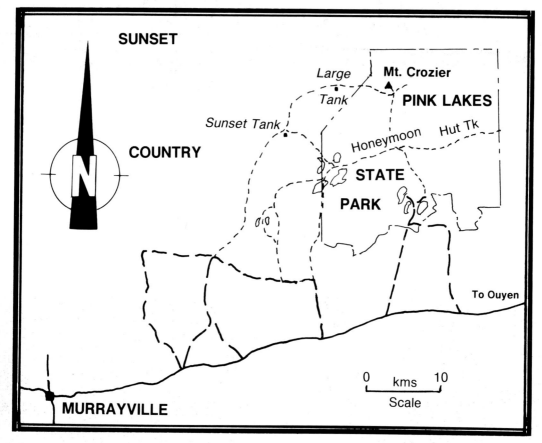

SUNSET

COUNTRY

*Large*
*Tank*

*Sunset Tank*

Mt. Crozier

**PINK LAKES**

*Honeymoon*   Hut Tk

**STATE**

**PARK**

To Ouyen

0   kms   10

Scale

**MURRAYVILLE**

**49.3 (9.9)**
Road on left — turn left onto dirt road.
Signposted (SP) 'Pink Lakes State Park'.

**49.4 (0.1)**
Cross railway line then cross roads — main
track veers slightly to right continuing
straight ahead.

**60.3 (10.9)**
T-junction — turn left. SP 'Pink Lakes State
Park'.

**60.6 (0.3)**
Track on left — PSA — SP 'Ring Road'.
Lake Hardy on right.

**61.6 (1.0)**
Y-junction — veer left.

**62.3 (0.7)**
Track on left — PSA. Lefthand (LH) track
leads to the camp ground. Lake Crosby on
left.

**63.8 (1.5)**
Track on right — continue on main track
which veers slightly around to left.
Righthand (RH) track leads to lakes. Lake
Crosby is quite a large lake. Very nice
camping throughout this area. Large cleared
areas with numerous trees.

**65.0 (1.2)**
Cross roads — turn right onto Ring Road
SP 'To Mt. Crozier Track'.

**65.9 (0.9)**
Y-junction — take main track veering to
right. Salt Bush Flat Track LH fork.

**66.9 (1.0)**
Leave the large cleared area and enter
bushland.

**68.7 (1.8)**
Signpost on left — PSA. To the right Lake
Kenyon, another large salt lake, and straight
ahead to Mt. Crozier.

**68.8 (0.1)**
Y-junction — veer left on Mt. Crozier Track.
Ring Road RH fork.

**69.3 (0.5)**
Sign on left — 'Deep Sand 4WD Only'.

**69.4 (0.1)**
Pass through gate. Track on right
immediately after — PSA.

**76.8 (7.4)**
Large cleared area which would make great
camping with quite a few large trees for
shade. There are a number of large pines
also through this area.

**79.7 (2.9)**
Large cleared area.

**81.4 (1.7)**
Y-junction — veer right.

**81.6 (0.2)**
T-junction — turn right. SP 'Mt. Crozier
Track' and 'Honeymoon Hut Track'.

**81.7 (0.1)**
Y-junction — SP 'Mt. Crozier Track'. Take LH fork. Large cleared area just after junction.

**87.4 (5.7)**
T-junction — turn left. RH track SP 'Management Vehicles Only — Walkers Only'.

**87.5 (0.1)**
Y-junction — veer left. LH track SP 'Mt. Crozier Track', RH track 'Mt. Crozier'.

Just 600 metres up the RH track will take you to the car park area for the walk up to Mt. Crozier with some great views of the surrounding area.

**89.9 (2.4)**
Cross salt lake area with what appears to be a dam on right.

**93.3 (3.4)**
Pink Lakes State Park sign on the right.

**95.3 (2.0)**
Cleared area — possible camp site.

**96.2 (0.9)**
Cleared area — possible camp site.

**96.7 (0.5)**
Dam or natural soak on left. Enter another very large cleared area.

**96.9 (0.2)**
Large dam on left — good spot for camping. Sign on left 'Mt. Crozier Track'. PSA.

**97.3 (0.4)**
T-Junction — turn left.

**97.6 (0.3)**
T-Junction — turn right. SP on left 'Large Tank'. LH track leads down to dam.

**99.7 (2.1)**
Old fence line and stock yards on left.

**103.5 (3.8)**
Track on right — PSA.

**106.7 (3.2)**
Monkey Tail Dam on right — SP — PSA. Cleared area around this spot.

**109.1 (2.4)**
Y-junction — veer right. SP 'Underbool Track' RH fork. Immediately after junction a track goes off to the left.

**111.4 (2.3)**
Track coming in sharply on right SP 'Grub Track'. Main track veers to the left.

**112.5 (1.1)**
Y-junction — veer left. RH fork is quite faint.

**114.0 (1.5)**
Track on right — PSA.

**115.1 (1.1)**
Track on right — PSA.

**118.0 (2.9)**
Pink Lake State Park sign on left.

**118.2 (0.2)**
Track on left — PSA.

**118.6 (0.4)**
Track on left — PSA.

**119.3 (0.7)**
Y-junction — veer right.

**120.2 (0.9)**
Track skirts salt lake area on left.

**121.4 (1.2)**
Track on right — turn right — SP 'Clay Lake Track'. Main track continues straight ahead.

**124.8 (3.4)**
T-junction — turn right — SP 'Clay Lake Track'. Pass through a large claypan area which has quite a bit of samphire.

**128.0 (3.2)**
Pass through fence line and gate.

**129.3 (1.3)**
Large salt lake on right.

**130.0 (0.7)**
Fence line and gate. SP on right — 'Pink Lake State Park'. Large salt lake area on the right.

**130.1 (0.1)**
T-junction — turn left. RH track leads down to another large lake area.

**132.2 (2.1)**
Salt lake on right with a cleared area.

**132.4 (0.2)**
Faint track on right — PSA. RH track leads 100 metres to a cleared area beside a salt lake. Red Lake is visible just over the hill from this spot.

**133.9 (1.5)**
Pass through fence line and gate. Farmland now on left.

**135.7 (1.8)**
Track on right — PSA.

**137.5 (1.8)**
Y-junction — veer right.

**138.1 (0.6)**
Faint track on right — PSA. Track has now improved to a wide, graded dirt road.

**138.7 (0.6)**
Pass through fence line and gate — PSA.

**140.5 (1.8)**
Track on right — PSA.

**142.7 (2.2)**
Pass through fence line and gate — PSA. Windmill and tank on right.

**143.7 (1.0)**
Track on left — PSA. Farmland on both sides of road.

**148.1 (4.4)**
T-junction — turn right onto bitumen — Ouyen Highway.

**183.8 (35.7)**
Murrayville Hotel.

# RUNNING THE BEACH —
# Millicent to Robe

Victoria is unlucky that its many beaches are out of bounds for four wheelers. Luckily though, just across the Victoria/SA border there is a beach run which has it all — remoteness, challenge and a wild, windswept beauty.

Long stretches of beach are interspersed by low rocky headlands and patches of half submerged reef. Waves roll in from the great Southern Ocean, tearing at nature's sandy battlements, and in the process changing the beach conditions along this stretch of coast. That means, no matter how many times you've been along here, you can always be surprised by the differences in sand and beach conditions.

Around every headland or where a patch of reef juts into the sea, huge middens of shells testify to the long existence of Aborigines on this coast. Most middens are now well marked and fenced for protection.

Wildlife is not brilliant, but occasionally you'll see a seal resting on the beach and with luck you'll be able to get quite close to him.

Bird life is never greatly obvious, but for those with keen eyes there are a host of feathery friends to attract the interests. Dotterals, terns, oyster catchers, gulls and other marine birds are the most common, but so are parrots, birds of prey and smaller bush birds. Many migratory waders can also be seen spending our summer far from their homes in Siberia or the Arctic. All in all over 200 species of birds have been recorded here.

## STANDARD
Medium to hard. You really should travel this route in the company of others — there's strength in numbers, and you'll almost definitely get bogged somewhere.

You'll need at the very least basic recovery gear.

Don't forget to lower tyre pressures — 15–18 psi is where you should start. You may have to drop them lower if you get bogged.

Numerous tracks are located along this route. Many are not mentioned in the trek notes. We've tried to keep them as simple as possible and included all the important track junctions and the like.

## DISTANCE and TIME

Millicent is some 470 kms (6 hours driving) west of Melbourne and 430 kms (5 hours driving) south-east of Adelaide.

From Millicent to Robe is around 110 kms. Allow at least a full day to drive it.

## RECOMMENDED MAPS/GUIDES

The South Australian National Parks and Wildlife Service has a brochure covering their parks in the area.

The best maps are from the AUSLIG 1:100,000 topographic series. You'll need Robe, Conmurra and Millicent. The South Australian Department of Lands also has a 1:50,000 series covering this area, but you'll need five maps to cover this region.

## CAMPING

Apart from the small towns along the way, a number of camping sites exist just inland from the beach. Lake George, north of Beachport, has a number of sites, as does the Little Dip area. No facilities exist. Carry out any rubbish and don't forget to take water.

## RESTRICTIONS/PERMITS REQUIRED

Stick to marked tracks. Erosion is a big problem through this area and many sea birds nest just above the high tide mark. Please don't disturb them.

## TREK

**0.0 (0.0)**
Pub in Millicent — proceed down North Terrace past the pub.

**0.7 (0.7)**
T-junction — turn right.

**0.9 (0.2)**
Track on left — turn left into Lowey Street and head towards the coast. Road is signposted (SP) to 'Safcol Factory'.

**5.3 (4.4)**
Cross Roads — proceed straight ahead (PSA).

**7.5 (2.2)**
T-junction — turn right. Lake Bonnie off to left.

**7.6 (0.1)**
Track junction — turn left onto Causeway Road.

**12.5 (4.9)**
Road turns to gravel.

**13.6 (1.1)**
Y-junction — veer right to Oil Square Rig Road.

**13.7 (0.1)**
Y-junction — veer right to Oil Rig Square.

**16.0 (2.3)**
Oil Rig Square — drive straight across and pick up the track on the other side.

**16.3 (0.3)**
T-junction — turn right. Warning sign for loose sand and dangerous rips.

**17.0 (0.7)**
Camping area on right — PSA to gap in sandhills. Camping area is desolate, but can handle big groups.

**17.2 (0.2)**
Up over sand dune and on to beach. Turn right.

**23.0 (5.8)**
Track turns inland to the right, crossing over sand dunes.

**24.3 (1.3)**
Cross rocky area — take care.

**24.9 (0.6)**
Cross roads — PSA.

**25.3 (0.4)**
Y-junction — veer left, continuing on main track.

**25.7 (0.4)**
Pass Aboriginal midden on left.

**25.9 (0.2)**
Cross roads — PSA on main road. SP 'Southend 9 km (straight ahead).

**26.1 (0.2)**
Y-junction — veer left.

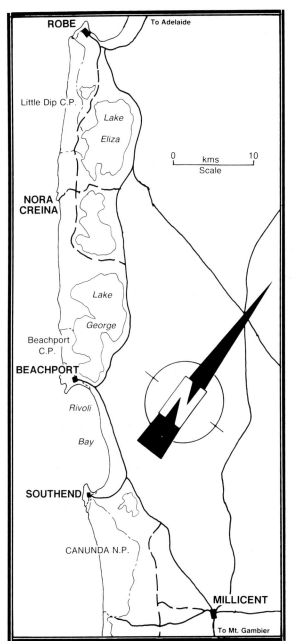

**26.6 (0.5)**
Y-junction — veer right. Lefthand fork goes down along the beach and it's very soft — beware of getting bogged and the tide coming in.

**27.0 (0.4)**
Pass around Aboriginal midden on right. Cliff edge on left. Now back into sand dune country — leaving the rocky sections behind.

**27.6 (0.6)**
Track on left — PSA on main track which winds through sand dunes. Lefthand (LH) track leads down to the beach.

**27.7 (0.1)**
Y-junction — veer left.

**27.8 (0.1)**
Track on left — PSA on main track which veers sharply right, up around over sand dune. The track continues inland now away from the beach through the sand dunes. LH track leads to the beach.

**28.1 (0.3)**
Follow fence line on right. Revegetated area behind the fence.

**30.1 (2.0)**
Track junction — veer left on main track. Track coming in sharply on right, SP 'Bevilaqua's Ford 9 km (to right)', beach to left.

**30.5 (0.4)**
Track on left — PSA. LH track leads to a camping area (SP as such).

**30.6 (0.1)**
Track on left — PSA. LH track leads into a large cleared area amongst the vegetation for camping (SP).

**31.1 (0.5)**
T-junction — turn right onto graded/gravel road. SP 'Boozy Gully/Cullens Bay' track on left.

**31.8 (0.7)**
Track on left — PSA. LH track SP 'Abyssinia Bay'.

**33.3 (1.5)**
T-junction — turn right onto bitumen road and cross the Lake Frome Outlet Drain. Enter Southend. Continue following the bitumen.

**33.6 (0.3)**
Road on left — turn left into Leake Street. SP 'To The Beach'. Follow the bitumen down to the beach.

**34.0 (0.4)**
Hit the beach — turn right. You're now on Rivoli Bay. This section of beach is also quite good for driving on. Very firm base with the tide out.

**46.6 (12.6)**
Good track on right leads up from the beach — PSA. This section of beach continues to be a good run — taking into account the tides.

**48.8 (2.2)**
Track on right — turn right up and over the dunes.

**48.9 (0.1)**
T-junction — turn left. Back on bitumen heading to the township of Beachport.

**50.3 (1.4)**
Sign 'Township of Beachport'.

**51.3 (1.0)**
T-junction — turn right. SP 'Five Mile Drift'.

**51.5 (0.2)**
Track on left — turn left into MacCort Street — Scenic Drive/Salt Lake. Continue following bitumen road.

**52.7 (1.2)**
T-junction — turn right into Bowman Scenic Drive. Back onto dirt. Follow main dirt road.

**55.2 (2.5)**
Track on right — turn right. The main gravel track continues straight ahead. This is an easy track junction to miss — look out for it.

**55.7 (0.5)**
Track on left — PSA through the sand dunes. The LH track leads down to the beach. This stretch of beach though is quite a tough section to drive along, especially if the tide is in.

**56.2 (0.5)**
Y-junction — veer left down to the beach. Back on beach turn right.

**56.6 (0.4)**
Track swings around to the right close to the headland — very soft sandy section.

**56.8 (0.2)**
Track swings off the beach back behind the dunes.

**56.9 (0.1)**
Track junction — PSA entering rocky sections. Track coming in sharply on right and track on left which leads to the beach.

**57.6 (0.7)**
Back on beach for a short distance.

**57.8 (0.2)**
Pass very large Aboriginal midden on left. Track goes right back into the dunes, meandering around midden.

**58.2 (0.4)**
Track on right — continue on main track which veers round to the left.

**58.3 (0.1)**
Track on left — veer right continuing on main track.

**58.8 (0.5)**
Faint track on right — PSA.

**59.3 (0.5)**
Track on right — veer left continuing on main track which soon drops onto the beach.

**60.3 (1.0)**
Track swings off the beach just before a headland into a large sand blow area. Track veers round to the left up a steep dune, follow track through the sand dunes.

**60.8 (0.5)**
Around here numerous tracks come in on the right from the sand blow area — can be used as a diversion around the steep sandhill.

**61.2 (0.4)**
Steep descent down onto the beach. This section can be a risky beach run at high tide.

**61.6 (0.4)**
Track on right leads up off the beach — turn right.

**62.7 (1.1)**
Just after a steep drop onto the beach is a Y-junction — take the righthand fork off from the beach.

**63.0 (0.3)**
Y-junction — veer left. Leads down onto the beach. Righthand (RH) track continues on behind the sand dunes. Fairly soft sand along this stretch.

**70.5 (7.5)**
Rocky Headland — track continues to the right around the headland and then back onto the beach.

**72.4 (1.9)**
Track swings back around another headland and then onto the beach again. There are quite a few steep pinches on the track around the headland.

**78.0 (5.6)**
Track on right — turn right. Track passes around a large rocky headland.

**78.2 (0.2)**
Enter the township of Nora Creina. Follow the main track through the township.

**78.5 (0.3)**
Track on left — PSA. LH leads back down to the beach to a beautiful little bay area with a couple of islands. Protected around front by a rocky headland and reef. However you can't actually drive around this beach area.

**79.0 (0.5)**
Leave Nora Creina and its 'Private Area' sign.

**81.1 (2.1)**
Cross roads — turn left.

**90.3 (9.2)**
Track on left — turn left into Little Dip Conservation Park past the sign.

**92.0 (1.7)**
Track on right — turn right up sandhill. Cleared area around this track junction is sometimes used for camping.

**92.2 (0.2)**
Track on left — PSA. LH track takes you over to the nearby headland.

**92.5 (0.3)**
Back onto the beach.

**93.2 (0.7)**
Track on right and orange marker — turn right heading off from the beach. The track is marked with orange stakes through this area.

**95.0 (1.8)**
Back on beach.

**95.6 (0.6)**
Track turns off the beach and heads inland. Quite a steep sandblow area through here so take care. The track once again meanders through thick vegetated dunes.

**96.2 (0.6)**
Track on left — turn left down onto the beach.

**96.4 (0.2)**
Tracks swings off the beach up near the orange poles.

**96.5 (0.1)**
Track on right — veer left, continuing on main track back onto the beach.

**96.7 (0.2)**
Exit track on the right — turn right.

**97.2 (0.5)**
T-junction — veer right. LH track leads to the beach.

**98.1 (0.9)**
Track junction — veer left and have fence on your right.

**99.4 (1.3)**
Y-junction — veer left towards beach away from farmland — orange pole marks the spot.

**100.0 (0.6)**
Track junction — turn hard right. Junction is just behind the first line of dunes — almost cross roads.

**100.5 (0.5)**
Big sand hill — the big one to test you is on the left. Easier track on right.

**100.9 (0.4)**
Track on left — veer left down towards the beach.

**101.0 (0.1)**
Track junction — PSA down to the beach. Track heads north behind the first line of dunes.

**102.9 (1.9)**
Move off the beach for a short distance skirting some rocks and back onto the beach.

**103.5 (0.6)**
Diversion on the right — exit track about 500 metres before you get to the headland — turn right.

**103.8 (0.3)**
Hit a large sandblow area and follow orange posts across the sandblow.

**104.8 (1.0)**
Drop over steep sandridge — it's the last big one on the trip before Robe.

**105.0 (0.2)**
Camping area on left and sign on right stating 'Vehicles must stay on defined track'.

**105.2 (0.2)**
T-junction — turn left onto main graded track.

**106.6 (1.4)**
Track junction — PSA into Robe. Back on bitumen. LH track leads to the rubbish tip. RH track leads to Beacon Hill Lookout.

**107.9 (1.3)**
Major cross roads. Now in the centre of Robe.

# ROCKY TRACK AND THE STEPS

This short trek is one of the hardest in the book. As such it is only for experienced drivers who have a well setup rig. For those who think the climb up Rocky Track is terrifying enough, then "The Steps" should be admired and left alone. It can be extremely dangerous.

The forests in this area consist mainly of messmate, manna gum and mountain grey gum, with an understorey of wattle, hazel pomaderris, ferns and bracken. Over 25 species of mammals have been recorded in the surrounding forest and 150 species of birds call the region home.

Wee Creek, followed and crossed on this trek, is a tributary of the Yea River which flows into the Goulburn, just north of the township of Yea.

## STANDARD
Hard to extreme. If it's wet "The Steps" can be extremely dangerous.

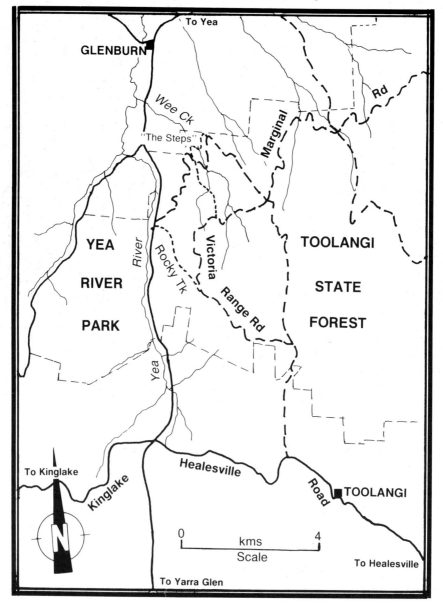

## DISTANCE and TIME

From Yarra Glen and return it is only 60 kms. Timing may only be an hour, but could be much longer.

The township of Yarra Glen is only 50 kms north of Melbourne and has all facilities.

## RECOMMENDED MAPS/GUIDES

The Conservation Forests & Lands 1:100,000 map Toolangi-Black Range is probably the best, although it does not show ''The Steps'' track.

## RESTRICTIONS/PERMITS REQUIRED

No restrictions exist on these tracks at present.

## CAUTION
Log trucks use many of these roads during the working week, while trail bike riders and four wheelers use them on the weekend. Take care.

## TREK

**0.0 (0.0)**
Yarra Glen, 50 kms from Melbourne, in middle of town, heading north.

**16.3 (16.3)**
Cross roads — PSA. Toolangi and Healesville to right, King Lake to left.

**21.4 (5.1)**
Yea River Park sign on left.

**22.8 (1.4)**
Track on right — turn right onto dirt track.

**22.9 (0.1)**
Cross roads — PSA, track signposted (SP) 'Rocky Track'. Righthand (RH) track SP 'Romix Track'.

**23.0 (0.1)**
Track junction (tracks left and right) — continue on main track (Rocky Track) which veers right up the hill. The climb up is fairly steep, rough and very rocky.

**23.7 (0.7)**
Over the worse of the steep and rough section of track.

**24.4 (0.7)**
Track on right — PSA.

**25.3 (0.9)**
T-junction with major track — turn left. Track you've just come up is SP 'Rocky Track'.

**27.5 (2.2)**
Cross tracks — turn left, SP 'Wee Creek Track'. There are a number of boggy sections along this track to negotiate — especially in wet conditions.

**28.7 (1.2)**
Faint track on left — PSA on main track which veers to the right.

**29.9 (1.2)**
Cross roads — turn left onto Marginal Road (SP) and then immediately turn right again onto track on right. Don't veer off to the left following Marginal Road.
Immediately after turning right off Marginal Road you have a Y-junction — veer right, heading steeply downhill.

**30.4 (0.5)**
Small creek crossing and then a small cleared area on the right — big enough for a small tent.
Just as you begin to climb up, out of the creek bed, you have the choice of either going left or right up the hill.
The lefthand (LH) track is very steep and eroded, with some exceptionally large 'steps' to climb up and over. It is an extremely difficult track to drive up.
The righthand (RH) track is again just as steep, but is not as difficult a climb, being mainly eroded and deeply rutted with a bit of loose rock making traction at times difficult.

**30.7 (0.3)**
Over the worse of the climb up.

**31.0 (0.3)**
Y-junction — veer right.

**31.1 (0.1)**
T-junction — turn right back onto Marginal Road.

**33.3 (2.2)**
Track junction — PSA on Marginal Road. LH track is SP 'Wee Creek Track', RH track leads back to the steep climb up the hill.

**36.2 (2.9)**
Track on right and large car park area — PSA. RH track SP 'Glenburn Track'.

**36.3 (0.1)**
T-junction — with Yarra Glen Yea Road — turn left for Yarra Glen.

# RUBICON TO TORBRECK

The headwaters of the Rubicon, Royston and Big Rivers, along with Snob Creek, were pioneered for grazing by a number of families who entered the area during the 1870's. Torbreck Station, established in the early 1890's and located near the junction of Running Creek and Big River, covered much of this area with sheep and cattle grazing south to Stockman's Reward.

In the 1920's the Rubicon and Royston Rivers were chosen as the site for the first hydro electricity scheme in mainland Australia. Opened in 1927, the scheme brought roads and tracks to this once remote region. Once producing up to 30% of the State's electrical power

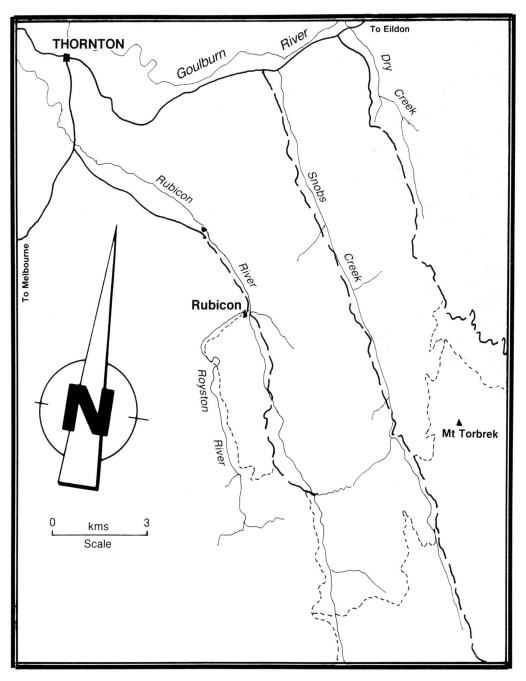

requirements, the scheme now produces less than 1%! However, its dams, aqueducts, power stations and small tramways are worth more than just a cursory look.

One of the reasons why this area was selected for a hydro scheme is that it is one of the wettest areas in Victoria. That rain not only supplies water to the dams, but can play havoc with the tracks in the area.

During the 1930's many small sawmills operated in the area and during the 1939 fires was one of the hardest hit regions of the State. Today scattered ruins and the occasional huge sawdust heap are mute testimony to the endeavours of these early timber workers. Presently, forestry is still carried on in much of the surrounding forest.

This trek takes you from Taggerty to Rubicon, up the Royston River Valley, across into the Rubicon Valley and then over the range to Snobs Creek. After crossing the creek the route skirts the flank of Mount Torbreck before heading north to Eildon.

Ferns, lush undergrowth, tall Mountain and Alpine Ash, along with Black and Silver Wattle and Sassafras combine to form a verdant cloak of vegetation across the ranges.

Wallabies are often seen, especially on the cleared grassy areas bordering the aqueducts, while Platypus can be seen in the rivers and deer seen in and around the dense forests. Birdlife is also varied, with Lyrebirds, Wonga Pigeons and other mountain loving birds being common.

## STANDARD
Easy to medium.

## DISTANCE and TIME
Taggerty is on the way to Eildon, about 120 kms (2 hrs drive) north-east of Melbourne. It is less than 80 kms from Taggerty to Eildon, with a driving time of 2–3 hours. You can make a good weekend out of it though.

## RECOMMENDED MAPS/GUIDES
AUSLIG 1:100,000 'Alexandra' or the 1:63,360 Forest Commission of Victoria 'Taggerty'.

## CAMPING
A number of camping sites exist along this trek. Most are along the Rubicon River or up on Barnewall Plain.

## RESTRICTIONS/PERMITS REQUIRED
The area is managed by the Conservation Forests & Lands and the State Electricity Commission of Victoria.

Some of the tracks are closed between June and the end of October.

There's no rubbish collecting services, so take all rubbish out with you.

## TREK

**0.0 (0.0)**
Y-junction — turn right into Taggerty. Junction of the Maroondah Highway and the Taggerty Thornton Road. This is the last place to get fuel and supplies at the General Store in Taggerty.

**10.7 (10.7)**
Road on right — turn right. Signposted (SP) 'Rubicon Road'.

**11.7 (1.0)**
Rubicon Valley Horseriding and Bicycle Hire facility, ph: (057) 73 2292, on right.

**15.8 (4.1)**
Bridge & gravel Road . Sign on right 'Sanctuary — Deer Hunting Prohibited'.

**16.7 (0.9)**
Track on left — PSA. Lefthand (LH) track leads to Kendall's Camping area on the Rubicon River. Along this stretch of road you'll find a number of tracks on the left which lead down to some nice camping along the river.

**18.7 (2.0)**
Track on left — PSA towards the Rubicon Power Station. LH track SP 'Royston Road', leads to some good camping just over the bridge.

**18.9 (0.2)**
Cross the Aqueduct Bridge. Road veers round to the left immediately after crossing the bridge, followed by an information sign on left which outlines the history of the Rubicon Hydro Scheme. Then cross another bridge over Rubicon River. The Rubicon Power Station is directly on the left. At this point the track veers to the right and continues past some houses.

**19.2 (0.3)**
Gate and sign 'Rubicon River Road' on right — PSA. Now following the Rubicon River on your right.

Depending on track condition this track could be closed, it is normally open from October and closed during the winter months. If so divert via the Royston Road, which will rejoin this trek at the junction of the Rubicon River Road and Royston Road.

**21.2 (2.0)**
Gate & track on right — PSA.
Travel through some very nice tree ferns and gums along this section of track.

**21.8 ((0.6)**
Good views of the Rubicon River Falls on right.

**22.5 (0.7)**
View of dam on right.

**22.9 (0.4)**
Faint track on left — PSA.

**23.0 (0.1)**
Old sawdust heap on right. Site of old sawmill — burnt out in the 1939 fires.

**25.2 (2.2)**
Gate — PSA.

**25.3 (0.1)**
Track on right — PSA. SP 'Tom Burns Road'.

**26.3 (1.0)**
Pass under power lines.

**26.7 (0.4)**
Pass under the old tramway bridge. Then have the aqueduct and old tram way on your right.

**26.9 (0.2)**
T-junction — turn left. Sawmill on right and house in front.

**27.1 (0.2)**
Power station on right.

**27.2 (0.1)**
Track on right — continue on main track which veers left.

**28.0 (0.8)**
T-junction — turn right onto Royston Road. SP 'Royston Road' and 'Rubicon River Road'.
  Note: This is the track junction where you would join this trek if the Rubicon River Road was closed and you diverted around on the Royston Road as mentioned earlier.

**28.4 (0.4)**
Bridge crossing the Royston Aqueduct.

**29.5 (1.1)**
Track on left — PSA. LH track leads down to the Royston Dam — 'No Entry'.

**30.8 (1.3)**
Faint track on right — PSA.

**33.2 (2.4)**
Y-junction — veer left.

**34.2 (1.0)**
Y-junction — veer left, continuing on Royston Road. RH fork SP 'Quartz Creek Road'.

**34.3 (0.1)**
Y-junction — veer left onto No. 5 Fire Track.

**35.1 (0.8)**
Track on right — PSA. RH track leads to an old boiler which is part of the relics of an old saw mill. Just after this junction there is a faint track on left. Continue on main track.
  Around this area you'll find an old sawdust heap and remains of relics of the past in amongst the bushes.

**35.3 (0.2)**
Track veers round to left and crosses the Royston River. There is a small camping spot on the right just before you cross the river. Once across the river there are a couple of old huts and horse yards and you'll find a few small camping areas. This area is used by the horse trail riders for their overnight stop.
  The track veers round to the right past the hut and horse yards.

**35.4 (0.1)**
Gate and cross Whiskey Creek. Steep climb out of the creek on an eroded track.

**38.0 (2.6)**
Logging area.

**40.4 (2.4)**
Track on left — PSA.

**43.5 (3.1)**
Camp area on right. Nice cleared area on the old Anderson Road along side junction of Snobs Creek and Bull Creek.

**43.6 (0.1)**
Wooden bridge and gate. Gate SP 'Closed until end of October'.

**44.0 (0.4)**
T-junction — turn left onto Snobs Road.

**46.6 (2.6)**
Track on left — PSA. SP 'Hobins Gap Road'.

**46.7 (0.1)**
Track on right — turn right onto Conns Gap Road.

**47.5 (0.8)**
T-junction — turn left.

**47.6 (0.1)**
Gate. SP on left '4WDs Only Beyond This Point'.

**49.1 (1.5)**
Barnewall Plains.

**49.3 (0.2)**
Camping area. Very nice designated camping area with fireplace and table — lack of water being the only problem. Walking track on right SP 'Mt. Torbreck Walking Track — Return Walking Time 2 Hours'.

**49.8 (0.5)**
Gate. Road improves.

**51.7 (1.9)**
T-junction — turn left onto Torbreck Road . SP on right 'Barnewall Plains Road & Torbreck Road'.

**56.0 (4.3)**
Cross Roads — turn left onto bitumen towards Eildon. SP 'Eildon 13 kms/Jamieson 51 kms'.

**71.3 (15.3)**
T-junction with Goulburn Valley Highway. Turn left for Melbourne (153 km) or right for Eildon (3 km).

# TOM GROGGIN TO BENAMBRA

Nestling below the main range of Mt. Kosciusko, Tom Groggin Station once used to straddle the Murray River. Today the New South Wales side is part of the Kosciusko National Park, but on the other side of the river Tom Groggin Station still survives, an island of freehold within the newly proclaimed Victorian Alpine Park.

This trek takes you from the camping area on the New South Wales side of the river, across the turbulent mountain stream that is the Murray at this point, up on to the Davies High Plains. This is one of the remotest regions in Victoria and the gnarled snow gums and spectacular scenery make this a delightful area for those wishing to get away from it all.

Brumbies will often be seen, and if you camp up in the high country the howl of a dingo will no doubt be heard.

From the great views of the High Plains the route drops you down onto the Murray once again at a spot called the Poplars or McCarthy's. From here you follow Limestone Creek south to Black Mountain Road and onwards to Benambra.

The scenery and the country is nothing short of spectacular. The camping is superb and the fishing can be great as well.

## STANDARD
Moderate to hard. The country is remote, so it's advisable to travel in company.

## DISTANCE and TIME
Tom Groggin is some 500 kms north-east from Melbourne and 8–9 hours drive. Benambra is 6 hours and 340 kms from the city.

From Tom Groggin to Benambra is around 105 kms. You'll need fuel for at least Corryong to Benambra, a distance of 200 kms.

You could do it in a day, but three would be a lot better.

## RECOMMENDED MAPS/GUIDES

The best map is the 1:100,000 Jacobs River available through AUSLIG outlets and good map stores.

## CAMPING

There are many pleasant places to camp — on the Murray at Tom Groggin, up on the high plains at a number of spots and on the Murray River at the Poplars.

## RESTRICTIONS/PERMITS REQUIRED

This region is closed off during winter as track closures close all tracks up onto the high plains.

Do the right thing. Keep on tracks. Take out all rubbish.

## WARNING

Even in summer bad weather can strike with rain, hail and even snow. Be prepared.

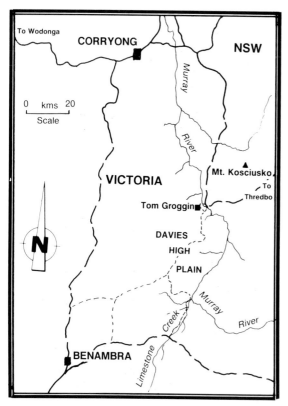

## TREK

**0.0 (0.0)**
Trek notes begin at the road junction right beside the sign of Tom Groggin Picnic Area and the Alpine Way, nearly 2.0 kms past Tom Groggin Station. Track leads south, through the picnic ground.

**0.9 (0.9)**
Camping areas alongside the river.

**1.0 (0.1)**
T-junction — turn left, skirting river.

**1.3 (0.3)**
Track on right — proceed straight ahead (PSA). Righthand (RH) track leads to camping area.

**1.6 (0.3)**
T-junction — turn right.

**2.4 (0.8)**
Rough descent towards river.

**2.5 (0.1)**
Murray River and crossing. River crossing is okay, the banks are a little bit slippery and a little bit lumpy — care required.

**2.6 (0.1)**
T-junction on the other side of the river — turn left.

**3.7 (1.1)**
Y-junction — veer right. Lefthand (LH) fork leads to Gauging Station.

**4.3 (0.6)**
Faint track on left — PSA.

**5.5 (1.2)**
Creek crossing. Couple of nice camp sites on the far bank.

**6.4 (0.9)**
Gate post where National Parks would close the road.

**7.4 (1.0)**
Fence line on right.

**8.5 (1.1)**
Small creek crossing.

**8.6 (0.1)**
Y-junction — veer right. LH track was old alignment.

**8.9 (0.3)**
Y-junction — veer left up steep hill. RH track was old alignment. Track climbs steeply from that point.

**11.2 (2.3)**
Skirt edge of creek.

**11.3 (0.1)**
Cross creek. Could be wet and boggy when there is a bit more water around. Nice camp spot just up from the creek. On climb up the hill from creek crossing there are numerous old tracks on the right of the current road.

**15.4 (4.1)**
Top of the range.

**17.4 (2.0)**
Faint track on left on small snow plain — PSA. Surrounded by snow gums. Since hitting the top of the range you pass through some areas of big, old gnarled twisted gums and snow gum country. Track junction is just off to the left of the small snow plain — good camping area.

**18.1 (0.7)**
Y-junction — veer right continuing on main track.

**18.2 (0.1)**
Break out onto large snow plain.

**18.7 (0.5)**
Cross Crystal Creek — beautiful mountain stream.

**19.1 (0.4)**
Track on right — turn right. LH track leads into cattlemen's hut through the fence line. Worth a look as the hut has a lot of character. Good camping.

**23.1 (4.0)**
Track on left — PSA.

**26.2 (3.1)**
Large area of snow plain which would make a good camp — great views to both sides of the range.

**26.8 (0.6)**
Snow plain — beautiful views.

**27.4 (0.6)**
Track on right — turn right, signposted (SP) 'Davis Plain Track'. LH track leads downhill to the river!

**32.0 (4.6)**
Creek crossing — bridged. This is also the area where the National Parks put their 'Road Closed' sign in.

**32.1 (0.1)**
Creek crossing. Beautiful camping spot.

**32.2 (0.1)**
Little causeway across a brook. Good camping.

**32.3 (0.1)**
Faint track on left — PSA continuing on main track.

**34.7 (2.4)**
Gate (which is closed at different times). Just past the gate are cross roads — turn left on to the McCarthy Track — past the 'Road Closed Barrier 2kms — June 15 — October 31' sign. RH track is Buckland track. Straight ahead is a fainter track which heads back to the Benambra Road.

**36.8 (2.1)**
Winter Barrier.

**40.3 (3.5)**
Faint track on right — PSA.

**43.6 (3.3)**
T-junction with the Limestone Creek Track — turn left to McCarthy's or the Poplars.

**44.1 (0.5)**
Track on right — PSA. RH track SP 'Helipad'.

**44.6 (0.5)**
Cross Murray River.

**44.7 (0.1)**
Poplars camp site. Spend some time here. Good fishing and exploring.
   To head to Benambra retrace steps across the river.

**45.8 (1.1)**
Track on right — PSA along Limestone Creek Track. RH track is McCarthy's.

**46.5 (0.7)**
Creek crossing.

**48.2 (1.7)**
Camp site.

**48.3 (0.1)**
Creek crossing. Just before creek crossing SP on right 'Cobras Tingaringy National Park'.

**50.6 (2.3)**
Creek crossing. Reasonable camp site.

**53.4 (2.8)**
Creek crossing. Reasonable camp site on left.

**54.2 (0.8)**
Small creek with a steep climb after it.

**55.5 (1.3)**
Track on right — PSA. RH track leads down to a good camping area on river flats.

**56.3 (0.8)**
Winter time barrier.

**57.1 (0.8)**
Small creek crossing. A number of camp sites around this area with tracks leading down to the creek.

**57.6 (0.5)**
Track on right — PSA. RH track follows creek giving access to good camping areas.

**57.8 (0.2)**
Track on right leads to a camping site.

**58.0 (0.2)**
Track on right to camping site.

**58.9 (0.9)**
Y-junction — veer left.

**60.0 (1.1)**
Track junction with Benambra Road — turn right for Benambra and Omeo. Good road from here.

**66.0 (6.0)**
Y-junction — veer left.

**67.0 (1.0)**
Y-junction — veer right.

**83.5 (16.5)**
T-junction — turn left and follow main road (good dirt and bitumen) to Benambra.

**99.5 (16.0)**
Benambra township.

# WARBURTON TO POWELLTOWN

This trek meanders through the hill country, south from Warburton to tiny Powelltown.

The magnificent forests in this region are delightful and offer a great escape from the city, virtually just a stone's throw away. Much of this country was burnt in the 1983 Ash Wednesday bushfires, so much of the smaller trees are regrowth from that time. In other areas huge gums, their thick trunks dominating the roadside, tower upwards. In spring there are many wild flowers to capture the senses.

Birdlife in the area is excellent, but you'll need to stop and look for it. The thick scrub holds many secrets, but if you take it easy and you're there early in the day or in the evening you'll possibly see lyrebirds, wonga pigeons, wrens and robins by the score, plus a host of honeyeaters.

There's no need to pack the camping gear for this trip — it can be easily completed in a day. There's a number of places where you can stop for lunch and the setup picnic area near the end of the trek is excellent.

From here there are a number of pleasant walks. Some of these follow the old logging tramways through the forest, and they offer an easy stroll through the heart of this verdant country. In fact, this picnic area is at the site of an old sawmill and nearby you'll see the huge sawdust heap where many forest giants ended their days.

While most of this trek is of an easy nature, there are some tough hills and tracks in this area. A good map will help you find them.

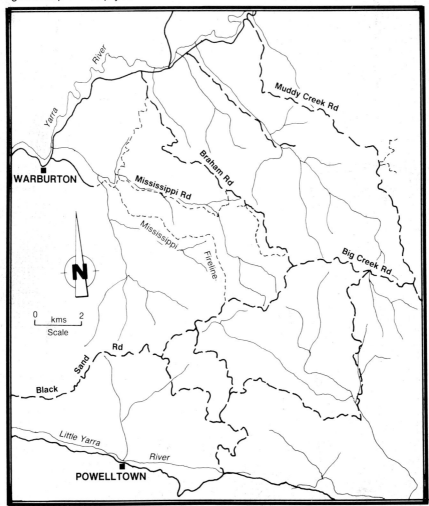

## STANDARD
Easy to moderate. Some of the tracks can be difficult if it's wet.

## DISTANCE and TIME
From Warburton to Powelltown is a 2–3 hour jaunt, if you don't stop.

## RECOMMENDED MAPS/GUIDES
The best maps to have are the 1:100,000 Healesville, and the Forestry map covering the same area.

## TREK

**0.0 (0.0)**
Warburton — Centre of town heading east.

**1.4 (1.4)**
Turnoff to Donna Buang on left. Proceed straight ahead (PSA)

**12.8 (11.4)**
Cross Starvation Creek — still on bitumen.

**16.1 (3.3)**
Track junction — turn right off main bitumen onto dirt. Signpost (SP) at the junction 'Registered Bikes and Licence Riders Only. No offroad riding'.

**17.1 (1.0)**
Cross roads — PSA.

**17.6 (0.5)**
Track off to left — PSA.

**19.7 (2.1)**
SM Track on right — PSA.

**23.1 (3.4)**
Muddy Ridge Track on left — PSA.

**23.6 (0.5)**
Faint track on left — PSA.

**24.2 (0.6)**
Major track junction — PSA. Starvation Creek Road on right.

**26.2 (2.0)**
Track on left — PSA.

**27.2 (1.0)**
McMahons Creek Road on left — PSA.

**27.4 (0.2)**
Road on left — 'No Through Road' — PSA.

**29.2 (1.8)**
Starvation Creek Track on right (blocked off) — PSA.

**30.7 (1.5)**
Major track junction — veer right. Brown's Road off to left.

**31.0 (0.3)**
Track junction — veer right.

**33.6 (2.6)**
Major track junction — veer right. McCarthy's Spur Road off to left heading towards Noojee. Big Creek Road off to right.

**36.1 (2.5)**
Federal Road on left — PSA.

**40.1 (4.0)**
Major T-junction — turn right onto Brahams Road.

**40.6 (0.5)**
Track junction — take centre track — No. 7 Track. Lefthand (LH) track is Oaks Spur Track. Far righthand (RH) track is main road.

**44.1 (3.5)**
Track junction with three tracks — veer right, not hard right.

**45.3 (1.2)**
Track junction — turn hard left into Mississippi Road.

**49.7 (4.4)**
Track junction — PSA. Track off on right.

**51.8 (2.1)**
Track junction — PSA on Mississippi Road. Lyre Bird Road off to right.

**52.2 (0.4)**
Mississippi Track on left — turn left. Quite a few steep climbs on Mississippi Track.

**57.3 (5.1)**
Track junction — PSA. Track off to right.

**58.7 (1.4)**
Centre of old logging coup loading area.

**60.7 (2.0)**
Major road junction — PSA onto Big Creek Road.

**61.9 (1.2)**
Major road junction — PSA towards Powelltown. Picnic area on left. From this picnic area you can take Smyth Creek Road back to where we started from. Excellent spot for a picnic or to take a walk.

**62.6 (0.7)**
Y-junction — take LH fork.

**67.3 (4.7)**
Cross roads — PSA.

**68.8 (1.5)**
Track junction — PSA.

**73.5 (4.7)**
Major road junction — turn right towards Powelltown — hit the bitumen.

**79.0 (5.5)**
Hit Powelltown. There is only a pub and a general store and a few houses.

# THE WESTERN GRAMPIANS

The Grampians are one of the most picturesque regions of Victoria. The area has long been recognised as a tourist destination, especially the magnificent ranges around the small, but expanding township of Halls Gap. Much of the region is proclaimed national park, however the area around Rocklands Reservoir, far to the west, remains forest reserve and/or State Park.

Here, along the shores of Rocklands and amongst the rugged bluffs of the Black Range, the country is more open. Possibly it is not as spectacular as the Wonderland Range near Halls Gap, but there are fewer people, the camping is excellent and the wildlife and flowers (especially during spring) are superb. In fact, the wildlife is so good we consider it the best we've seen in Victoria — by a long shot.

To the east of Rocklands are the towering peaks and bluffs of the Victoria Range. Many people, ourselves included, consider this range to be the most spectacular in the Grampians. There are some magnificent rock formations that are well worth a walk to. Castle Rock, or the Fortress, as it is also known, is probably the best known, but the "Hole-in-the-Wall", described in these notes, is a fantastic formation. The walk is harder, but the view is great.

These Trek Notes take you from Dunkeld on the Glenelg Highway, to Balmoral, onwards to our favourite places along the shores of Rocklands. From here many excursions are available, but these notes continue north around the reservoir onto the Henty Highway for a short distance and then around and up the rugged spine of the Victoria Range. From here the notes head to Glenisla Crossing and then eastward through the heart of the Grampians, across the eastern ranges south of Halls Gap, back to Dunkeld.

## HISTORY

Used by Aborigines for generations, Sir Major Thomas Mitchell became the first European to see and explore the area in 1836. By 1840 most of the good farming land had been taken up and it wasn't long before the Grampians started to gain their reputation as a great place to visit. In fact, the area was being advertised as a holiday venue as early as 1868.

The many man-made lakes that are now so much a part of the Grampians scheme owe their existence to the work begun in the 1880s. Water was scarce in the drier regions to the north and west of the mountains, so a system of dams and open channels were constructed to supply these areas with essential water. Now the 10 lakes and the 8300 kms of open channel that supply 49 towns and 7000 farms in the western districts make it the biggest system in the world. Rocklands Dam, the largest in the system, was completed in 1953 and covers over 6500 hectres, offering fine camping along much of its shore line, as well as some good fishing.

### Aboriginal Art and Shelters

Many Aboriginal art sites are located throughout the Grampians. Most of the well known sites are protected by ugly, but seemingly necessary, wire mesh. If you find any unprotected by mesh please do not touch. They are not only fragile, but also Victoria's only Aboriginal art. Don't expect the glory of northern Australian Aboriginal art. The sites in the Grampians are older, far more fragile and more weathered.

## STANDARD

Easy. Only the section along the Victoria Range Road comes close to real 4WD. The track along the range is rough and severely eroded in places.

## DISTANCE and TIME

Dunkeld is around 260 kms west of Melbourne and a 3–4 hour drive from the city.

From Dunkeld to Dunkeld via the trek notes it is around 280 kms, but there are so many options available you could make it shorter or much longer.

For most people the Grampians are a weekend or longer trip.

The trek as described would be a long day's drive. Hence we'd recommend camping at the spots detailed so you've got the time to enjoy the bush a bit. Allow plenty of time for any drive along the Victoria Range.

## RECOMMENDED MAPS/GUIDES
The best single map is the Conservation Forests and Lands map called 'The Grampians'. This map is available from the Department of Conservation Forests and Lands, Victoria Parade, Melbourne, or the Melbourne Map Centre or Bowyangs, Kew.

A couple of books that are ideal travelling companions are "The Grampian Ranges by Road & Track" or "50 Walks in the Grampians".

## CAMPING
You can camp at the dam wall of Rocklands if you'd like a few facilities. A camping and caravan ground is located there along with a boat ramp. There is a small kiosk at the camping ground, alternatively the nearest stores and facilities are available at Balmoral.

The western shore of Rocklands has a host of areas for bush camping. We generally stay up near Mountain Dam Creek which has long been a favourite with us.

Buandik Camping Area is also an excellent place to camp. The surrounding forest is magnificent and the Victoria Range is just a stone's throw away.

## RESTRICTIONS/PERMITS REQUIRED
Some of the tracks through the Grampians are subject to seasonal closure over the winter months. The Goat Track and Victoria Range Track are closed off between the 1st July and the 30th September. Harrop Track is the alternative in these notes (between 150.5 and 188.6), it is a good road, but you miss out on the best of the drive. Other tracks could also be closed and the dates could be extended — it depends on the season. Check with the Department of Conservation and Lands, Horsham, ph: (053) 82 5011.

## Camp Fires —
The Grampians are a high risk area for bush fires so please ensure adequate precautions are observed when using a camp fire in the region.

## TREK

**0.0 (0.0)**
Dunkeld Township. Continue west along the Glenelg Highway.

**3.5 (3.5)**
Road on right — turn right to Cavendish. Mt. Sturgeon and Mt. Abrupt rise steeply from the flat plain to the north.

**31.0 (27.5)**
Cavendish Township. Follow sign to Balmoral — turn right.

**32.5 (1 5)**
Y-Junction — veer left, following signs to Balmoral and Rocklands Dam.

**70.5 (38.0)**
Balmoral Township & Crossroads — proceed straight ahead (PSA). Balmoral has all facilities.

**71.5 (1.0)**
Glenelg River — bridged — PSA. Good birdlife often seen in swamp, to the right of road.

**81.5 (10.0)**
Road on left — turn left. Straight ahead leads to Rocklands, the dam wall and the caravan and camping ground.

**82.2 (0.7)**
Track on right — turn right off bitumen and head into forest.

**88.7 (6.5)**
Track on right — PSA. Righthand (RH) track leads south and eventually reaches edge of reservoir.

**93.5 (4.8)**
Track on right — PSA. RH track leads to Mountain Dam Creek camping area. Good camping along edge of reservoir.

**93.6 (0.1)**
Mountain Dam Creek crossing.

**101.5 (7.9)**
Track on left — PSA. Lefthand (LH) track, known as Muirfoot Track, leads through Black Range.

**101.8 (0.3)**
Mouchong Creek crossing. Caution on creek crossing — it can difficult.

**101.9 (0.1)**
Y-Junction — veer left.

**106.9 (5.0)**
Track on right — turn right — H.G.H..
Corner. Straight ahead leads to Black
Range Camping Area and Aboriginal art
galleries. The camping area has no water.
Excellent short walks in the area,
magnificent caves and great views.

**113.6 (6.7)**
Track on right — PSA. RH track leads
south to upper reaches of Rocklands Dam.

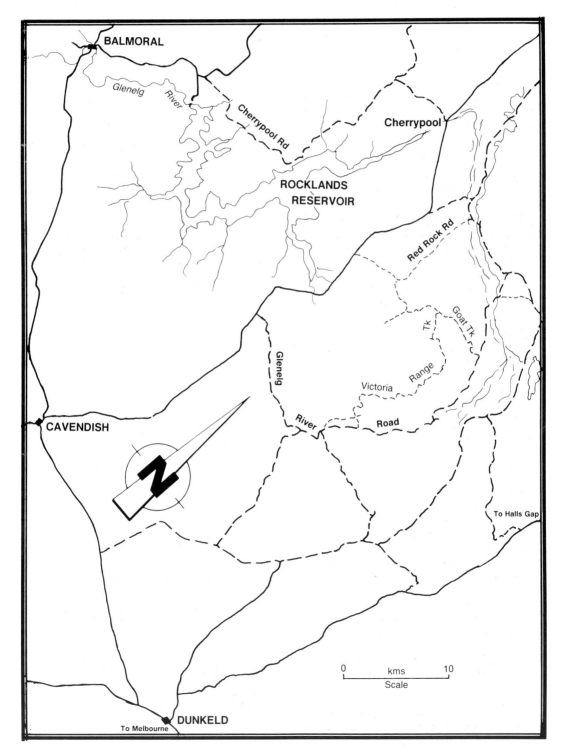

**114.1 (0.5)**
T-junction — turn right heading south along Highway. Hit the bitumen of the Henty Highway at Cherrypool. Directly opposite the road junction are picnic and toilet facilities along edge of Cherrypool — a beaut place to swim and watch the birds. Some hides for observing the water birds have also been erected around to the left of the facilities.

**144.3 (30.2)**
Cross Roads — turn left. SP 'Glenelg River Road'.

**145.8 (1.5)**
Track on right — turn right. LH track now permanently closed.

**150.5 (4.7)**
Cross Roads — PSA. North-south running track is Harrop Track.

**155.9 (5.4)**
Chimney Pots Camping Area on right, just off main track — PSA. The formation known as the Chimney Pots are directly to the north. Track winds for a short distance past this point.

**157.4 (1.5)**
Track on right — PSA. A hard right turn leads back along Bullawin Road to Victoria Point and eventually to Dunkeld.

**159.9 (2.5)**
Track on right — PSA. RH track is Jensens Road.

**160.2 (0.3)**
Track junction — veer right, keeping on Glenelg River Road.

**163.7 (3.5)**
Cross Road — turn left.

**164.0 (0.3)**
Glenelg River crossing — upper reaches. Track begins to climb, slowly at first then more steeply and deteriorates.

**165.2 (1.2)**
Track junction — PSA. Sawmill track crosses track. Gate 100 metres further on is closed during winter.

**169.2 (4.0)**
Track junction — PSA. Track alternates between reasonable slow going to plain rough.

**170.5 (1.3)**
Track on left — PSA following the top of the range. The going is generally slow. LH track leads downhill for about 800 metres. A half hour walk along a faint track from this point leads to Castle Rock, or the Fortress. It is worth the trouble.

**175.5 (5.0)**
Track on left — PSA, beginning to descend range — often badly eroded. LH track is a 20 minute walk to Mt. Thackery.

**182.0 (6.5)**
Track on left — PSA, track beings to improve. LH track is Hut Creek Track — permanently closed. However, along this track is a pleasant 6 km walk to Harrop Track, meeting the track about 4 kms south of Buandik. This track also gives you the easiest access (although shorter from the Harrop end) to the 'Hole-in-the-Wall' — a rock formation south-east of the junction of Hut Creek and Hut Creek Track. The last stages of this walk are difficult.

**184.4 (2.4)**
T-junction — turn left onto the 'Goat Track', and degenerates quickly as it climbs, then descends the range.

**185.7 (1.3)**
Track on right — PSA. RH track is SP 'Cave of Fishes Walking Track', which leads a short distance to the Aboriginal art site known as 'The Cave of Fishes'.

**188.3 (2.6)**
Track on right — PSA. RH track leads into the Buandik Camping Area. An excellent spot to camp. No pets allowed. This spot is rarely crowded. Nearby is the Glenisla Shelter which contains one of the most extensive amounts of Aboriginal art in the Grampians.

**188.6 (0.3)**
Cross roads — turn right onto Harrop Track. Track straight ahead leads into the heart of the Billywing Plantation.

**188.9 (0.3)**
Cultivation Creek.

**191.2 (2.3)**
Track junction — PSA.

**191.9 (0.7)**
T-junction — turn right onto Red Rock Road. LH track takes you on Billywing Road to the Henty Highway. If you are travelling this road in the evening the ranges to the east look dramatic.

**201.9 (10.0)**
Road junction — turn right onto Lodge Road. LH road leads to Glenisla Crossing.

**202.9 (1.0)**
Moora Irrigation Channel.

**203.1 (0.2)**
Track junction — PSA. If you are travelling this road in the early morning the red bluffs to the south-west look great.

**208.1 (5.0)**
Round Swamp — on left of road.

**208.7 (0.6)**
Cross roads — turn right down Syphon Road. Airstrip on left. Normally lots of kangaroos and even Emus around here, especially in the morning and evening.

**211.1 (2.4)**
Track junction/Moora Irrigation Channel — turn hard left and follow Mair's Track

northwards. The continuation of Mair's Track that follows the channel is closed to vehicles. Mair's Track can be wet and boggy.

**214.6 (3.5)**
T-junction — turn right onto Lodge Road again.

**217.2 (2.6)**
Road junction — turn right onto Glenelg River Road.

**218.4 (1.2)**
Track on left — PSA. LH track is Hennam Track.

**222.3 (3.9)**
Moora Irrigation Channel — PSA. Moora Moora Reservoir lies just to the left (east) of the road. A number of pleasant picnic spots — just off the road — are passed along this section.

**229.6 (7.3)**
Cross roads — turn left onto Serra Road.

**241.8 (12.2)**
Track junction — PSA. Hennan Track crosses Serra Road at this point. Road climbs from this point.

**242.8 (1.0)**
Teddy Bear's Gap.

**245.1 (2.3)**
Dunkeld-Grampians Road junction — turn right (south) for Dunkeld. Hit the bitumen at this point. Left leads to Halls Gap (22 kms).

**248.1 (3.0)**
Road on left — PSA. LH road is Jimmy Creek Road. On right is Jimmy Creek Camping Area — a popular pleasant camp on the Wannon River. As you head south you travel along the eastern edge of the Serra Range.

**255.1 (7.0)**
Road junction — PSA. Wannon camping area on left on Wannon River.

**257.1 (2.0)**
Road junction — PSA. Mirranatwa Gap to right.

**274.1 (17.0)**
Cross Roads — PSA. Cassidy Gap Road to right.

**278.6 (4.5)**
Track on right — PSA. RH track leads to picnic area and beginning of walk up Mt. Abrupt. It is steep, but the views are good.

**281.1 (2.5)**
Road junction — turn left. On your right, just after the intersection, is the beginning of a walking track up Mt. Sturgeon. Once again good views of the surrounding area.

**283.9 (2.8)**
Dunkeld/Glenelg Highway. Turn left for Melbourne.

# THE WONNANGATTA VALLEY

The fabulous Wonnangatta Valley is one of the great 4WD destinations in Australia, and it's in Victoria!

Completely surrounded by mountains, the Wonnangatta was the "Lost Valley" of the Alps. First discovered by A.W. Howitt during his wanderings through the high plains looking for gold in 1860, Wonnangatta Station was taken up soon after, probably by the American prospector Oliver Smith. John Bryce entered the scene soon after, taking over the lease around 1866.

In 1917–18 the infamous "Wonnangatta Murders" took place. Today the murderers of James Barclay, the then current leaseholder and his cook John Bamford, is still not known. Some say Bamford, in one of his angry argumentative moods, killed Barclay, and then a friend of Barclay's (he had many) killed Bamford. Others thought both were killed by rustlers. We'll probably never know, but it all adds to the beauty, mystery and character of this hidden valley.

The first vehicle to enter the valley was in 1945 when a horse track was widened to take the legendary Harry Smith to Sale. Harry, who was 98 and son of the American Oliver Smith, had lived all his life in and around the valley and was one of the great horsemen of the region.

The original homestead built by Smith and enlarged by the Bryce family was accidentally burnt, probably by bushwalkers, in May 1957. Sold a number of times after the death of the last Bryce family member, the station freehold land was finally purchased by the Victorian Department of Conservation Forests & Lands in 1988. Today, as part of the Alpine National Park, it is a popular 4WD, camping, bushwalking and deer shooting area.

While it does get busy on summer long weekends, its many secluded camping sites along the river ensure an enjoyable stay.

## STANDARD
Moderate to hard. With its many river crossings, steep hills and unpredictable alpine weather this route, at times, can be extreme, hence its closure over winter.

## DISTANCE and TIME
While Dargo is some 300 kms east and 4–5 hours from Melbourne, Licola is closer at around 250 ks and 4 hours drive from the city.

Total driving time as follows —

Dargo to Wonnangatta Station Site — 3 — 3½ hours
Station Site to Howitt Plain Road — 2 — 2½ hours
Junction on Howitt Plains Road to Licola — 1¼–2 hours.

You could do it in a day, but the reason for going there is to enjoy the valley. Stop awhile!

Total distance of this trek is a little less than 200 kms. Fill your tanks at Dargo.

## RECOMMENDED MAPS/GUIDES
1:70,000 Crooked River-Dargo and Macalister River Watershed maps by S.R. & P.N. Brookes.

The book "Wonnangatta Moroka National Park" by John Siseman gives a lot of additional information to this region.

## CAMPING
There are many places to camp within the valley. All with varying degrees of access to the river.

## RESTRICTIONS/PERMITS REQUIRED
The area is managed by Conservation Forests & Lands and is declared national park region.

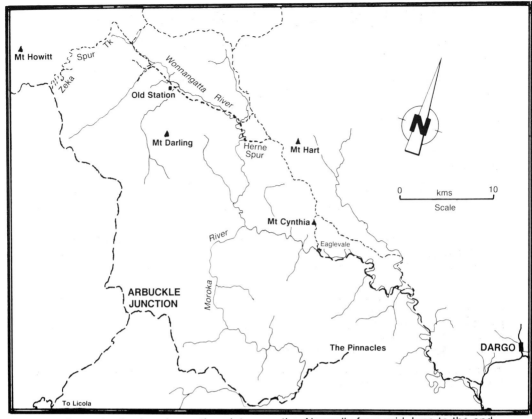

Access to the region is closed over the winter months. Normally from mid June to the end of October.

Stay on marked tracks and keep away from prohibited ones.

Ensure you take out all rubbish.

Obey all National Park regulations and observe fire bans and any requests by rangers.

# TREK

**0.0 (0.0)**
Dargo Pub — heading south.

**6.1 (6.1)**
Track on right — turn right off the bitumen, SP 'Short Cut Road'. Dirt track begins and crosses narrow bridge. The track junction is right on a bend 'Exhibition Corner' — turn with caution.

**8.3 (2.2)**
T-junction with Crooked River Road — turn right, heading towards Kingwell's Bridge.

**29.6 (21.3)**
Track on right — PSA crossing Kingwell's Bridge. RH track is Conway's Track, leading to Crooked River.

**35.5 (5.9)**
Track on left — PSA continuing north-west on Wonnangatta Road. LH track is Billy Goat Bluff Track.

**36.3 (0.8)**
Track on right — PSA. RH track leads towards the river.

**38.6 (2.3)**
Track on right — PSA. RH track leads towards the river.

**38.9 (0.3)**
Alpine National Park sign on left.

**42.8 (3.9)**
Alpine National Park sign on right.

**43.2 (0.4)**
Track on right on edge of cleared area — PSA. RH track leads towards the river and possible camping sites.

**44.3 (1.1)**
Y-junction — veer left. RH fork leads into private property.

**46.3 (2.0)**
Track on right — PSA. RH track SP 'Private Road — No Entry'.

**50.7 (4.4)**
Track on right — PSA on main track which veers to the left. RH track leads into private property.

**51.2 (0.5)**
Track on right and cleared area — turn right, SP 'Eaglevale Track'.

**51.6 (0.4)**
Footbridge and track on right beside the PMG Cable sign. Turn right and drop down into the Wonnangatta River, crossing to the far side.

**51.7 (0.1)**
Climb out of river and turn left, following track which runs alongside the private property and farmhouse on the right.

**51.9 (0.2)**
Footbridge on left and begin to climb towards Mt. Cynthia.

**52.3 (0.4)**
Track on right — PSA. RH track follows fenceline.

**55.5 (3.2)**
Alpine National Park sign on left on top of Mt. Cynthia. The climb up to Mt. Cynthia is quite steep, and the last 100 metres is extremely steep.

**56.0 (0.5)**
Track on left — turn left, SP 'Wombat Range'. SP also for 'Eaglevale Track/Cynthia Range Track'.

**62.1 (6.1)**
Y-junction — veer right. LH fork leads to Mt. Von Guerard.

**63.7 (1.6)**
Track on left — PSA.
The track is in good condition, with some excellent views of the surrounding mountain ranges. Also travel through some magnificent Mountain Grey Gum stands.

**68.8 (5.1)**
Y-junction — turn left, SP 'Herne Spur/ Steep Descent/Dry Weather Only'.
The next three kilometres are straight down. The track is good, but the descent is very steep and would be extremely difficult to negotiate in wet conditions, as would all the tracks in this region.

**72.0 (3.2)**
Faint track on left — PSA. LH track leads towards river. Now at the bottom of Herne Spur and entering the Wonnangatta Valley.

**72.3 (0.3)**
First crossing of the Wonnangatta River and gate. Gate would be closed during the winter months.

**73.2 (0.9)**
River crossing.

**73.9 (0.7)**
River crossing.

**74.7 (0.8)**
River crossing.

**75.6 (0.9)**
River crossing and small camp site on right just after crossing.

**75.9 (0.3)**
River crossing.

**76.0 (0.1)**
T-junction — turn left towards Wonnangatta Station. SP 'Wonnangatta Station' (to left)/ 'Wombat Spur' (right)/'Herne Spur'.

**76.1 (0.1)**
River crossing.

**76.4 (0.3)**
Track on right — PSA. RH track leads to a reasonable size camp site on river.

**78.2 (1.8)**
Numerous diversion tracks around a boggy, deeply rutted area.

**78.4 (0.2)**
Faint track on right — PSA. RH track leads towards the river.

**79.5 (1.1)**
Small creek crossing in swampy area.

**82.8 (3.3)**
Old apple trees marking the site of an old settlement on left — PSA.

**83.2 (0.4)**
Track on right — PSA. RH track leads to the river and camp site, 200 metres in from the track. Good access to the river.

There track along the section from the junction of Wombat Spur and Herne Spur is quite deeply rutted in sections. During wet conditions this area obviously becomes quite boggy, making driving very difficult.

**83.6 (0.4)**
Track on right — PSA. RH track leads to river and camp site.

**84.2 (0.6)**
Small creek crossing.

**84.6 (0.4)**
Site of the Wonnangatta Station on left — marked by a large stand of exotic old trees. There's some nice camping in amongst the trees, with a small creek running behind the tree line.

**84.7 (0.1)**
Large stand of old trees on left — part of the Wonnangatta Station site. Again, some very nice camping in amongst the trees, offering plenty of shade, with creek.

**84.8 (0.1)**
Cross creek bed (normally dry during summer months).

**84.9 (0.1)**
Track on left and remains of old cattle yard — PSA. LH track leads past the yards to an old hut.

There are numerous tracks around the homestead site and hut.

**85.2 (0.3)**
Cemetery on left, about 100 metres from the track — marked by a fence and a large old pine tree — PSA on main track.

There are numerous tracks in this area, however follow the main track for a about 500 metres past the cemetery, then veer left, up and over a small hill and continue following the track along the river flats.

**87.9 (2.7)**
Track on right — PSA. RH track leads towards the river.

**88.1 (0.2)**
Faint track on left — PSA.

**88.2 (0.1)**
Creek crossing (normally dry during summer months).

**88.7 (0.5)**
Cross Zeka Creek and track on left after crossing — PSA. LH track is the Zeka Creek Track — now closed to vehicles.

**88.9 (0.2)**
Track on left — PSA following track along river flats. LH track is SP 'Howitt Plains' and is an alternative route along the hill side, out of the river flats, joining the Zeka Track a few kilometres further on.

**92.1 (3.2)**
Y-junction — veer left, out of valley. SP 'Myrtleford' (to right)/'Wonnangatta Station'. RH fork is a continuation of the Wonnangatta Track.

**92.4 (0.3)**
T-junction — turn right onto Zeka Track. SP 'Howitt Road' (right)/'Wonnangatta Station' (to left). (Rejoin the alternate route SP 'Howitt Plains' at 88.9)

**93.8 (1.4)**
Small creek crossing — bridged.

**96.4 (2.6)**
Track on right — PSA. RH track SP 'Closed to all Vehicles'.

Up to around 11 km mark the track is very steep and rocky in sections, but the track is reasonably good.

**103.1 (6.7)**
Track improves, following the ridge line and then begins to slowly descend.

**107.6 (4.5)**
Small creek crossing — bridged.

**108.6 (1.0)**
Track on left — PSA. LH track SP 'Zeka Creek Track/Track Closed'.

**109.9 (1.3)**
Track on right — PSA.

**111.1 (1.2)**
Track on right — PSA.

**115.1 (4.0)**
Nice views out to left overlooking mountain ranges.

**115.2 (0.1)**
Gate and enter snow plains.

**115.4 (0.2)**
T-junction with Howitt Road — turn left to Licola and follow main dirt road south. SP at junction 'Zeka Track to Wonnangatta Valley — 4WD'.

**140.9 (25.5)**
T-junction — Arbuckle Junction — turn right for Licola.

**189.2 (48.3)**
Road junction — turn right for Licola. General store, fuel, camping ground. Turn left for Heyfield and Traralgon.

# SOUTH AUSTRALIA/VICTORIA BORDER FENCE

This trip is an interesting 4WD sojourn south from Murrayville in western Victoria, on the Ouyen Highway, to Bordertown, in South Australia, on the Dukes highway. It basically follows the old border fence that modern technology now reckons is in the wrong place and it should be a hundred metres or so further west. It seems SA will loose a little more land.

Initially, and at the end, the trip passes through wheat and sheep country. This gives way to the more natural heath and mallee country that once clothed vast areas of this part of Australia.

Sand plains and ridges clothed in a thick covering of vegetation stretch as far as the eye can see. The heath and mallee heath areas contain a wide variety of shrubs such as the desert banksia, scrub Cypress pine, she-oaks, tea-trees, grass trees, plus numerous smaller scrubs. In the taller scrub, mallee, Cyprus pine, broom heath-myrtle, broom bush (both once used widely for brush fencing) and tea-tree predominate.

In places amongst this wide swath of sand and thick vegetation, red rocky cliffs appear and this trek passes close to Red Bluff which is worth a visit. In other places natural clearings or areas where Cypress pine dominate make a pleasant change to the sea of mallee and heath.

As the trek progresses down the fence line it passes from one conservation park to another. On the South Australian side there is the Scorpion Springs Conservation Park which leads into the much larger Ngarkat Conservation Park. The area around Scorpion Springs itself is a naturally cleared area and is an excellent spot to camp. On its south eastern corner of Ngarkat is the Mt. Shaugh Conservation Park.

Over on the Victorian side is the vast Big Desert Wilderness which has on its south western flank, the Red Bluff Nature Reserve. Here an access track takes you into Red Bluff itself, where there is a reasonable camping area.

Along the way the keen eyed traveller will see a host of bird. Some 90 odd species have been recorded from the area, among which are the extremely rare Western Whipbird (more often heard than seen) and the Bustard. For reptile fans the area is rich in lizards and snakes.

Small mammals are only found by the most diligent, but the area around Red Rock and the Big Desert Wilderness is where the small, but very ferocious Ningauis were first recorded in Victoria. Larger mammals, such as Grey Kangaroos are often seen in the cleared areas.

In recent years the South Australian 4WD Association has been doing a lot of revegetation and track work in this area in the hope that such efforts will be rewarded with continual access. Don't stuff up there good work!

It is also advised that the Track be traversed north to south - the way these notes describe.

## STANDARD

Fairly easy, but there are a few sand ridges which may give some people a little trouble.

There are a number of ways to get on and off the Border Track, we've just detailed one of these, which also happens to be the best one if there has been heavy rain in the region.

The track is very remote for this region of Australia and little traffic uses it. Be prepared!

The best time to travel this area is late winter/early spring. Summer is unpleasant.

## RECOMMENDED MAPS/GUIDES

The best maps available are the 1:250,000 'Naracoorte' and 'Pinnaroo'. These cover the South Australian side of the border, so if you want the Victorian side you will need 'Ouyen' and 'Horsham', in the same series.

## CAMPING

Red Bluff and Scorpion Springs would be the best spots to camp, although there are many places that would be suitable.

Don't forget, there is virtually no ground water in this region, so take all you require with you. In summer the area is very dry and hot!

There are no facilities south of Murrayville, until you get to Bordertown.

## RESTRICTIONS/PERMITS REQUIRED

To get onto and off the Border Track the route passes through private land. Leave any gates as you find them, leave all stock and water points alone and respect the rights of the property owner.

For most of the way you're passing through conservation park of one sort or another. That means no guns or shooting.

Keep on the tracks provided and obey any other regulations imposed.

It is also advised that the track be traversed in the way detailed - that is, from north to south.

That way there is no danger, or at least, less danger of a head-on!

## TREK

**0.0 (0.0)**
Murrayville Hotel - heading east.

**0.4 (0.4)**
Road junction - Turn right (TR) - Road signposted (SP) 'Nhill 150kms' and to 'Lutheran Church and RCA Patrol Depot'.

**3.2 (2.8)**
T-junction - TR onto dirt.

**6.7 (3.5)**
Cross roads - Proceed straight ahead (PSA).

**10.6 (3.9)**
Cross roads - PSA.

**13.9 (3.3)**
Cross roads - PSA.

**20.4 (6.5)**
Cross roads - PSA

**23.1 (2.7)**
Cross roads - Turn left (TL)

**27.3 (4.2)**
Track junction - PSA.

**29.7 (2.4)**
Track junction - PSA.

**29.9 (0.2)**
Track on right - PSA. Track on right leads to Bulloak Well H.S. Road condition deteriorates.

**31.4 (1.5)**
Track on right - PSA.

**31.7 (0.3)**
Gate and fence line.

**32.9 (1.2)**
Gate and fenceline with track on left - PSA. Still passing through farmland.

**34.3 (1.4)**
Gate and fence line - PSA.

**34.4 (0.1)**
Track on left - PSA.

**34.8 (0.4)**
Track passes through border fence and large gate and then veers left with fence on right.

**35.3 (0.5)**
Gate and fence line.

**37.8 (2.5)**
Gate and fence line - PSA.

**38.1 (0.3)**
Track junction - TR away from Border Fence.

**39.4 (1.3)**
Cleared area with some old water tanks on right.

**39.8 (0.4)**
Large cleared area. Very nice camping here. PSA.

There is a track on your right which swings to the north and a sand-blow area just to the north-east. Pass a metal picket on your right and head towards a large sand-blow area which can be seen on front, keeping it to your left. Scorpion Springs nestles below this area about 100 metres from the junction.

**40.0 (0.2)**
Track on right - PSA.

**40.9 (0.9)**
Nature Reserve sign on left - now leaving Scorpion Springs C.P.

**43.9 (3.0)**
Track on right with windmill on left - PSA.

**44.1 (0.2)**
Track on right - PSA.

**45.8 (1.7)**
Faint track on left - PSA.

**46.1 (0.3)**
Track on right - PSA. Track on right leads to a unique hand dug well which is extremely deep, just 300 metres from track junction. There is quite a few large Cypress pines around this area, making it a reasonable spot to camp - no water.

**47.2 (1.1)**
Cross roads - TL

**52.0 (4.8)**
Track on right - PSA

**67.4 (15.4)**
Track on right - PSA.

**73.7 (6.3)**
Cross roads, marked by a tin on a stick - TL.

**80.5 (6.8)**
Fence and track on right - TR and follow
Border Fence south.

**90.3 (9.8)**
Old tin shed and faint track on right - PSA.

**94.4 (4.1)**
Faint track on right - PSA.

**100.1 (5.7)**
Border Fence Track passes through old
fence line and gate, track on right - PSA.

**101.2 (1.1)**
Faint track on left - PSA.

**102.1 (0.9)**
Track on left - PSA. Left hand track leads into
Red Bluff - SP 'Red Bluff Reserve'.

The carpark at the base of Red Bluff is
3.2kms from this junction. There is a
reasonable camping area here and great
views of the surrounding bush from the Bluff
itself.

**108.9 (6.8)**
Track on left - PSA. Begin to enter grazing
land and leaving the last of the biggish sand
ridges behind.

**111.5 (2.6)**
Track on left - PSA.

**118.3 (6.8)**
Old Border Fence line on right. Begin to pass
through farmland on both sides of track.

**124.4 (6.1)**
Track junction - TR. Now leaving fenceline.

**129.8 (5.4)**
Road on left - PSA.

**132.5 (2.7)**
Cross roads - PSA with slight dog leg to left -
bitumen road begins.

**140.3 (7.8)**
Road junction - TL - straight ahead leads to
Keith.

**159 4 (19.1)**
Enter Bordertown.

**165.9 (6.4)**
Road junction - TR.

**166.3 (0.4)**
Road junction - TL then immediately right
onto highway.

**167.3 (1.0)**
Bordertown.

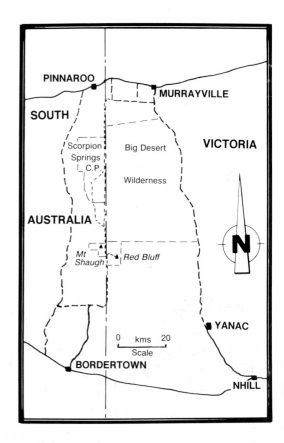

# SELECTING A TENT

**EDITORIAL. From the Age, Saturday 14 March 1992**

IF THERE is one thing which sorts out the men from the boys it is the task of selecting a suitable tent when four-wheel driving. The great majority of tents available in Australia are imported from Taiwan, China, Korea and Europe, with some coming from America.

Most buyers assume, incorrectly, that all tents are waterproof — they are not. They are usually either water-resistant or water-repellent, which is very different from being water-proof.

Many buyers, having already assumed the tent to be waterproof, then make another error in buying for appearance and, as imported tents are usually brightly coloured, they purchase for looks rather than performance.

Most imported tents fulfil at least a couple of the prime requirements, such as being relatively lightweight and, sometimes, also waterproof. But most are not easy to erect.

After a tough day of four-wheel-driving, the driver does not need the chore of setting up a large tent with ridgepole, fly, tent pegs, end posts, and so on.

The staff of '4 x 4 Australia' magazine have settled on the Freedom Minit Camper as being one of the most acceptable solutions. Made from waterproof and "breathable" Birkmyre Bivouac canvas, the tent can be erected in about one minute, using only four pegs and a centre-pole. It has a super tough vinyl floor, flexible fibreglass flywire windows, substantial zippers and, importantly, Freedom's factory guarantee.

Unlike most tents, these Freedom units are specifically designed to suit our weather conditions. All major stress-points are reinforced with canvas, nylon or leather, and use poles for instant, correct height adjustment, while seams are lockstitched.

## LOCATIONS

**VIC: FREEDOM CAMPING (Head Office)**
640 Elizabeth St. Melbourne. 3000.
Tel: (03) 347 7700 Ph/Fax: (03) 347 7946

**ACT: ARB CORPORATION**
85 Newcastle St (Fyshwick) ACT 2609
Tel: (06) 280 7475 Fax: (06) 239 1124

**NSW: TOWN & COUNTRY (UV4)**
Cnr King Georges & Moorefields, Beverly Hills. 2209.
Tel: (02) 758 2500 Fax: (02) 759 2649

**TAS: MAX STRATTONS**
80 Reiby St. (Ulverstone) 7315 Tel: (004) 25 1968

**QLD: AUSSIE TRAVELLER (Brisbane)**
51 Prospect Rd. Enoggera 4051
Tel: (07) 855 1066 Fax: (07) 855 1023 (008) 77 7625

**CAMPING GALORE (Townsville)**
225 Charters Towers Rd. 4810
Tel: (077) 75 3533 Fax: (077) 75 5344

**WA: GO CAMPING**
9/58 Erindale Rd Balcatta W.A. Tel: (09) 344 6252